LEAD WITH LOVE

LEAD WITH LOVE

A COLLECTION OF STORIES TO
HONOUR A MOTHER'S JOURNEY

LESLEY ANN FARIA ADAMO • SUSAN BAKER
NICKI DI GRAVINA • JANICE LAI YEE NG • EDEN PEREIRA
NICOLE RECKER • JESSICA RICHES • MARNIE SIGMAR
STEFANIA TERSIGNI • RUTH SCHALKHAUSER TOWER

LEAD WITH LOVE
A Collection of Stories to Honour a Mother's Journey

COVER DESIGN & BOOK DESIGN BY Jazmin Welch
EDITED BY The Studio Press
PUBLISHER The Studio Press

ISBN 978-1-7771734-3-2

To you,

May this book give you permission to lead with love.

contents

The Fire Within

JANICE LAI YEE NG

I am a mother. I am a wife. But who am I really?

Motherhood is a very interesting journey. For me, it's been a journey of rediscovering myself in a whole new world. A journey that is both so exciting and happy, but yet so lonely and sad.

Love and emotions. I never knew my heart could grow so much more and that I am capable of loving my kids this much. So much that it hurts at times.

Every milestone brought me a roller coaster of feelings. There was so much joy in watching them grow and experience things for the first time, but yet so sad seeing them grow out of their baby clothes, losing those chubby baby cheeks and becoming their own independent person.

But, somewhere along this journey, my identity shifted. And I felt lost.

I've always believed that motherhood is a choice and a responsibility that I have chosen to take on. So, I will love them with every ounce of my heart and soul, pour everything in through the sleepless nights and exhaustion. My life became about them and less about me.

But I wondered. Does motherhood define me? Who am I outside of identifying myself as a mother?

PIECES OF ME

I've always been a perfectionist. Growing up, I was taught to listen and to do as I was told. Expressing our feelings, emotions and asking questions was not a thing for my family.

So much that had happened in my childhood shaped who I became. I had watched my mom do everything for everyone at home without hesitation. Never once complaining until she became really sick and told me what she had gone through.

She passed away when I was seventeen. One of the last memories I have of her left me with a huge impact. I will never forget when she came home one day and told me that the doctor had said to us that we should take a family vacation. It was her way of telling me that her time was running out. She passed away soon after. We never did go on that family vacation.

As a mom, I feel nothing should stop me from doing all I can and more for my children. I am that mom who will attempt every Pinterest cake and every craft my kids want. I will go out of my way to create every possible experience with them that they can look back on. I am that mom who will go anywhere and everywhere with them, even when nobody else is up for it other than myself and the kids.

Life is short anyway, so why not now? Why wait?

I strive for perfection in everything. Perhaps I was seeking validation that if I were perfect, everyone would be proud of me and not worried about me. Maybe I was trying to make up for something my mom had missed out on.

ROCKING MOM

If anyone asked me, I would always say I was happy.

The new chapter of being a new mom was very exciting. Having grown up in Malaysia, I feel very fortunate to live in Canada, a country where I have the privilege to have one-year of maternity leave to watch my son grow. I did so much in that first year of motherhood. I took my baby everywhere, from coffee shops to business appointments. I was so content with this new way of life. I had a stable full-time job, a fulfilling wedding planning business on the side and a social life. What's not to be happy about?

But the truth is, every night, there were little voices in my head. My baby was growing up, and I had these weird inkling feelings in my heart. I obsessively looked at his newborn pictures every night before I slept, wondering where time had gone. I wished I could stop the time and put the newborn moments into a capsule and relive them over and over again. I always felt as if time was running out because life just seemed too short.

When the year passed, and it was time to go back to work, I began experiencing separation anxiety. I had just spent one whole year being with my child around the clock. I saw and listened to every little thing he did, but now this was being taken away from me. My baby was my life, and I was afraid to lose any time with him.

People told me that it would get easier, and to be honest, I never got used to it. Instead, I often cried while driving to work or back. I had to convince myself that that's just what life was, and there were no other choices.

When I was pregnant with my second child, this emotional struggle started to escalate differently. While my first pregnancy was so exciting with everything new and fresh, this time around was filled with worries and anxiety.

The pregnancy didn't come easy. It came with some complications. I was told that my baby was not growing at the rate he should be and that there were some growth restrictions. Maybe it was the hormones, or perhaps it was the weight that all mothers feel. I was carrying life inside me, and the responsibility that came with that was so big.

Every day I doubted myself.

What if I couldn't carry my child well? Why is my child growing at a slower rate than he should be, according to my midwives and doctors? Maybe I am doing something wrong. Maybe it's the food I eat. Maybe it's the exercise I do, or maybe I don't do enough.

As it got closer to birth, I thought, *can I love two kids the same way? Can I split my time with everyone? How do I make sure my kids and husband are happy?*

There was a strong need for me to compensate for whatever lack of attention my toddler was experiencing during this pregnancy.

No pregnancy, stress, or pain would stop me from giving him equal attention, if not more! I would take my son to different places to spend time with him doing fun things, even when there were times I could barely walk and was in pain.

To my baby, who was coming soon, he too deserved the best. So I set out to do all the things that I associated with loving my unborn child. I moved furniture myself, redecorated the nursery, sewed baby clothes, shoes and handmade toys. Despite how much pain and discomfort I was in, I would never complain. After all, isn't that how all moms are? We, as women and moms, just make it happen no matter what. We just do!

There were so many things I struggled with quietly the second time around. The exhaustion of having a baby that barely slept, cried constantly and trying to give my all to everyone else in the house. Everyone needed me all the time, but no one gave me a real break. A break isn't about going to the grocery store or taking my son out for a playdate.

My body. My feelings. My needs. I gave 100% to motherhood and nothing to myself. My every move was calculated because I thought that my role as a wife and mother should be.

I go through motherhood the way I was taught. I was there to serve my family the best I could. I was perfect, and I didn't need to spell it out if I needed help.

This only led to a lot of resentment towards my husband, who I felt didn't have to go through all of the changes that I had to. My life had changed, and while his life did too, it wasn't nearly to the same degree as mine had.

He didn't need to wake up every other hour or so. He was able to sleep through everything because he needed to go to work the next day. He didn't have to tend to a baby alone who cried all day long. He came home from work to get snuggles. He didn't have two children that wanted and needed him all the time.

At this point, my body didn't even feel like it was mine anymore. My body was designed to feed my babies and provide comfort. The children always needed me. They were always by my side, touching me and calling me. I wanted to yell and shove everyone away. I wanted to tell everyone to leave me alone and not talk to me, but at the same time, shouldn't I be thankful for all I have?

Motherhood is hard. My rollercoaster of emotions was so high and so low at the same time.

How do I split myself into pieces? How do I please everyone?

Because I've experienced the loss of my mom, I was so afraid of losing precious moments with my kids as they grew. All I knew was that I needed to give my all emotionally and physically. I felt guilty every time I needed space of my own. Everyone's needs trumped mine. I wanted to be there for everyone, do everything for them, fix everything and make everyone happy. I wanted to be the mom that does everything for her kids. I wanted to be the wife that makes sure her husband comes home from work to a tidy house and food on the table.

I was consumed by it all. The battle of voices filled my head. *I'm not a good enough mom. I'm not a good enough wife. I'm just not perfect enough. I'm not doing enough. I should do more. I'm running out of time, and I'm not spending enough time with everyone.* But, I was so tired. There was always sadness etched deep into my heart, and I was too often filled with guilt. I felt lonely in these thoughts.

CHASING STORMS

Through all this, I had always thought my wedding business gave me an outlet for all my anxiety and negative thoughts. Connecting with people who shared their love stories with me and helping them bring their vision to life made my heart sing. It brought me new experiences. It was my way to connect with myself besides being a mother and a wife and away from a full-time job that didn't provide me with that.

As the kids got older, my son would ask me, "oh, you're working again?" if I had to work on the weekends. I was always filled with guilt inside my heart for not being there for my child and leaving them to my husband or in-laws to help.

Between that and my husband's busy work schedule, I started to think. Would I want my kids to not see both parents on the weekend all the time? Do I want to spend all summer working away? I loved my wedding business, but I felt that I needed to apologize for anything I did related to it. I felt that I was not entitled to feel and to want things for myself.

My thoughts went back and forth with negativity. I can be more than this, but I am not. I am just a mother. I am a just wife. I am just an employee at a corporate job I didn't love. That was it. I didn't even know who I was anymore.

It became an endless cycle. *Am I a bad mom and wife if I want to continue my business? Am I a bad mom if I am so tired mentally that I don't want anyone to talk to me? Am I a bad person if I don't want to tend to my kids or husband? Am I bad if I want some space for myself?*

People told me that something had to go, that I just couldn't have everything. I was so confused. To give up something I love doing for my family or to continue doing it with guilt? I chose family.

I gave my business up and quietly became depressed. The business was all mine and just mine, and so I felt I lost a part of myself. But I kept telling myself that my kids were more important than my little side hustle.

As time went by, I started to feel disconnected from my body. I felt like a robot going through the everyday motions of a mother and wife. I felt sick every time I ate. I felt somewhat lifeless. I had been powered by perfectionism and anxiety. I made sure everybody else's needs were taken care of before my own. I was exhausted beyond words and didn't know how to express all that I felt. I didn't think anyone would understand this.

What was my purpose? Surely there is more to it all.

Some people told me that what I needed was to slow down. To stop doing all the things that kept me busy. That being so busy was the reason why I was feeling the way I did. Maybe that was it!

So I believed what everyone else told me instead of searching inwards.

I got to a breaking point where I started to seek some therapy. My soul needed more clarity. My heart needed more connection.

Then something happened.

When my son entered grade one, he often came home to tell me he was alone at recess and that he played on his own. Finally, after a lot of prompting, he told me that he was different from the other kids. He felt he wasn't good enough in school and couldn't run and jump like the other kids. He didn't want to play with other kids. My heart instantly dropped. Since becoming a mom, they were my priority.

Have I failed him? Have I forgotten what I thought I've done best as a mom?

I dedicated my nights reading up on what I could do to help him foster a better mindset. I read articles, I read forums, and I browsed the internet for ideas.

One day, after trying many different things and after many frustrations, I decided to have affirmation cards created with him on my mind. I didn't want to just buy a set of cards. I wanted them to be fully from me. I wanted this so much for him, and his brother as my greatest hope for my kids was for them to grow up to be good, happy and positive people. I nourished their soul and nurtured their happiness. Somehow, this little idea eventually grew into a small business.

What I didn't realize through this creation was that, in return, it nourished my soul. It gave me a purpose.

One day, my son came down in the morning and told me, "Mama, you are a genius." I asked why? He said to me, "You thought no one would buy your cards, but you believe in yourself!"

Oh, my heart!

This isn't a story about how I started my shop or how many cards I have sold. It was his words of believing in yourself that struck me. It was everything that I had been trying to teach him. And now it was my seven-year-old teaching me.

SHOW ME THE STARS

Answering the "Who am I?" question and rediscovering my inner self was indeed an eye-opening process.

I lost myself in motherhood somewhere along the way because I was too busy tending to other's needs, worrying about what others had said to me and pleasing everyone but myself.

My son's words brought it all back to me.

I forgot that I was capable of creating my own beliefs. Society taught me that as a mother, I must slow down and sacrifice for my family to be happy.

What if I didn't need to slow down like others thought I should? What if multitasking and having a million other projects is what fuels my soul? What about doing the things I love because I AM my own being instead of just putting everyone else first?

So I forgot.

I forgot what it was like to believe what I can be, give myself space, and love myself first. To stand up for myself and be who I am.

Having a business or doing something different, that I'm passionate about, does not make me less of a mom and wife.

My kids gave me a different purpose in life, but the shop gave me what I was searching for. A special connection with people I craved. Stories to share and learn from each other.

Deep conversations with my little kids. And through it all, I realized this is the best kind of teaching I can give them. I was their real-life example.

By showing up for myself, I am showing my kids what loving yourself is. I am strong. I am capable. I am more than just a mom. I am not a super mom, but I am an amazing mom. I was their hero by just being myself!

I have learnt that perfectionism doesn't quite exist. The victory is the bravery of recognizing and acknowledging failures within myself, then picking myself up and moving forward.

The connection with the outside world other than home brought me satisfaction and inner joy. This was my kind of self-care and self-love. I realized that I can still be myself while holding space for my family. I didn't always need to race against time and solve everyone's problems.

So, I am not just a mother. I am not just a wife. I'm much more than that!

And my purpose? To inspire my children, not just by loving them, but by teaching them to celebrate all the things that make up who they are.

Life is short, so I remind myself of this now. Find something that fulfills you. Do it. And do everything in between. So, when you take your last breath, you can say life lived.

So start living. Start creating. Start loving. Start inspiring.

Motherhood can be all of it.

The Space Between

MARNIE SIGMAR

On September 11, 2001, we left home at 9:15 am for Prentice Women's Hospital to have our baby just as the second tower of the World Trade Centre was hit in Manhattan. We were living in downtown Chicago where the city was working at blinding speeds to shut everything down. The fear was thick and palpable. The Sears Tower, just blocks away, could be the next target.

CONTROL

I had lists for everything. I had elaborate systems for crossing completed items off my list, ways of carrying forward the bazillion things I should have done and hadn't, lists for long-term projects, lists for the I-absolutely-have-to-do-this-today things. My lists made me feel prepared for everything. They were the assurance that I was in complete control. My lists got me from where I was to where I needed to be. There wasn't anything to worry about—it was covered on a list.

Best laid plans.

Getting pregnant was a major stumbling point on the life-planning list. Alex and I had been married for five years and living in Chicago for seven. I was no spring chicken. We wanted to create a family of our own. That was 1998. Not quite a year later, we started fertility treatments. The medication prescribed to me didn't help and instead made my chances of having a baby dwindle because of the damage it did to one of my ovaries. After staying the course for seven months, feeling completely defeated, I decided that I had to stop. I was shattered.

To fill the emptiness, I turned to making a new list. I decided I would take a year to do things that I couldn't do if I were pregnant. It was a way to switch the narrative completely. I decided to run the Chicago marathon and travel to Africa. Training for the marathon was therapeutic. Following a running schedule was the structure I needed. The training list had dates and times to run, dates to lift weights and dates to rest. The rhythmic beats of my running shoes hitting the pavement moved me forward. I completed the marathon and felt stronger and healthier than I ever had. Shortly after, we booked a trip to Africa and scheduled appointments to start Malaria medication and get our Yellow Fever and Hepatitis inoculations. In December of 2000, I had blood tests to clear the way to the first Yellow Fever shot. On December 23, I received a call saying that I would need to postpone my inoculations: I was pregnant. Check. Double-check. It might have been the most incredible news of my lifetime! I was pregnant. I was elated. Floating. Massive inhale. My heart expanded. I placed my hands on my stomach. *Could I feel a flutter in my belly?* I could already imagine this truth.

The following months were amazing. I created pregnancy lists and new baby lists. I stocked up with baby supplies and books. I bought books to prepare for pregnancy and birth, like "*What to Expect When You're Expecting*" by Heidi Murkoff. I also bought favourite children's books that I couldn't wait to read to our baby, like "*Goodnight Moon*" by Margaret Wise Brown, "*Guess How Much I Love You*" by Sam McBratny and "*Time for Bed*" by Mem Fox. I soaked in the wonder of the changes my body was going through. I caught myself rubbing my belly all the time. My side profile brought me instant joy. I immersed myself in the hopeful happiness that came with every phase of the pregnancy. I felt fantastic. I didn't have any cravings or food aversions but ate ice cream as if I did! Chubby Hubby. Tiger Tail. Chocolate Chip Cookie Dough. I was healthy, huge and knew in my heart from the very start that everything was going to be okay. This was it. I was going to have a baby.

I was due August 26 but, when that time approached, there were no signs of labour. Though my pregnancy was considered high-risk, there was no indication that we needed to hurry the process. I loved being pregnant. I loved feeling all of the baby's movement, more and more pronounced with time. My doctor was comfortable letting me go two weeks past my due date but no longer. And so, we were scheduled to be induced on September 11. By that date, I was the size of a Volkswagen. We had a shortlist of names for a boy and a girl. I savoured the time I had to set up the nursery. I took my time folding each little sleeper carefully, kissing the soft jersey sheets before tucking them around the corners of the mattress, rocking in the cozy rocking chair, imagining what it would be like. I finished setting up the baby's room with photos of four generations of our families, ready to surround our baby with love. Our nest was complete.

SURRENDER

The morning of September 11, we were ready. All lists were in order. Our hospital bag was perfectly packed, and the dogs had been walked. We were beyond excited. Just as we were getting ready to head out the door, a friend called to say that we needed to see the news.

Everything changed. The world stopped.

8:46 am the North Tower of the World Trade Centre was hit.

9:03 am the South Tower was hit.

We were in the midst of the single most deadly terrorist attack on US soil. I had no list for this.

Unmoored from my lists, I surrendered to the moment. I was fully present. I found myself in the space between what I expected to happen and what was actually happening. The space between is less about moving through and more about being. It is surrendering from the idea of what you should be doing to what is. Surrendering blueprints of expectation and response. It is not intuitive but rather a silent, invisible pivot into the moment.

That morning, it was the space between seeing the world unfold on the news and driving to the hospital. The space between was listening to my heart pound a little bit differently. It was the self-soothing, hands wrapped gently around my tummy, telling myself that we were going to be okay, repeating it silently. It was moving through the unknown, driving through the always congested city with no other cars on the streets. It was my husband's calm and steady pace navigating our entrance to the centre of the city. The intersections were blocked by police and emergency vehicles with flashing lights. I felt like we were sole survivors in a world no one else had seen. The space between was a slow-motion glance up at the Sears Tower against the backdrop of the bluest, clearest sky.

9:30 am we arrived at Prentice Women's Hospital.

On our way to registration, we met a nurse pacing the hallway, phone to her ear, who was desperately trying to reach her boyfriend in Manhattan. She couldn't get through to him. We tried using my cell. We tried using my husband's cell. All cell towers were down. I couldn't get close enough to her to give her a bit of energy, courage or comfort. I could feel her fear and wanted to do something, anything, to help. We kept trying though we all knew we wouldn't reach him. The space between was a departure from the task at hand to standing alongside this terrified woman. Fear. Disbelief. Heartache. Anguish.

9:37 am the Pentagon was struck.

I could feel all of the energy around me. Frantic. Scurrying. Worried expressions on faces we passed. Hushed voices. Loud television reporting. I could feel millions of hearts reacting to what was unfolding in our perfectly imperfect human ways. I was trying to sort everything that was happening in my mind. I wanted time to slow down to give me an opportunity to make eye contact, to offer words of comfort. I wanted to give more love than death could take. This situation was like no other we had known, and we were all going through it together but feeling so isolated in our experience. *How will this affect my family? Who do I know in Manhattan?* I remember visiting the Twin Towers. *What would it look like if Chicago was hit next? Would my baby be okay?*

The administrative staff and nurses were matter-of-factly doing their jobs, checking off their lists, directing us where to go. They must have been reeling inside, trying to reconcile all that was happening around them in real-time. They must have been wondering where their families were and how all of this would affect them. Grief. Responsibility. Shock. Sorrow. Preparedness. Care.

9:59 am the South Tower collapsed.

10:07 am Flight 93 crashed, intended to hit the Pentagon.

Our doctor, who had been with us throughout fertility treatment and this pregnancy, approached me as soon as we reached our room. She, normally pragmatic and sharp, was unravelled. She explained that she had to leave to be with her children. Apologetic, unapologetic. Understood. There is no judgement in the space between.

10:28 am the North Tower collapsed.

Everyone was frozen, glued to the images on every television screen. *Could this actually be happening?* Enormous chunks of cement and glass and people fell into heaps of mourning. The towers where firefighters rushed in to save people who were trapped were obliterated. The sky was raining paper and the stories of those who went to work that morning. People near the towers were running for their lives to beat the growing mass of debris. Shock and disbelief weighed on the faces of helpless bystanders who, just moments earlier, watched people in the towers cling tightly to each other at the edge of windows begging for help and dodging the scorch of the fires closing in on them. Each image hung in the air as if waiting to land somewhere sensible. I could hardly breathe. My legs couldn't hold me.

Would Chicago be hit next? We were close enough to the Sears Tower to be affected. My thinking was disjointed. What world was I bringing our baby into? Where was my family? Was my sister with her boys? I knew my mom and dad were on their way here from their cottage on Charleston Lake in Canada (probably listening to Johnny Cash—I can hear the deep hum of my dad's voice) with no sense of the world turned upside down until they were close enough to see how empty the city was. I had asked them to drive into a country under attack.

1:15 pm I was induced.

For hours, we were closed off from most of the rest of the world. Everything was blurry. My mom arrived at the hospital. My husband and my mom tried their best to inject levity. I couldn't bear to see news coverage of the attacks. Hospital monitors in our labour and delivery ward showed babies delivered and beds cleared. Nurses rushed in and rushed out; doctors started and finished shifts.

Emotions flowed through me like a swift current. Fear and excitement, knowing and not knowing, feeling and needing to stay focused, staying attached to the narrative that I was in control and letting go. I became aware of the space that existed between contractions with wonder, no expectation of what it would feel like next.

4:00 pm the following day, a doctor determined that I needed to have a C-section.

I was disappointed. I was relieved. I was groggy. I remember the anesthesiologist moving me down the hallway to a surgical room. He laid his hand on the top of my head and acknowledged that it was his second shift since I had been induced and I must be exhausted, as was he. Another moment of humanity and connection in the midst of the steady beat of hospital efficiency ramping down the chaos and uncertainty of the attacks. The space between slowed this transfer from room to room allowing me to feel supported. The space between allowed the comfort that came with his kind, calm words. Thoughtfulness. Generosity. Compassion.

6:46 pm Joe was born.

Everything changed. Our world changed. The world had changed.

Time stood still. My heart was suspended in the space between Joe's birth and moving to recovery, seeing my husband's face the first time he held our son. So much love. I had never seen life so clearly. I could feel our hearts beat.

Over the course of the next forty-eight hours, Joe was passed from person to person like sunlight on water. Everyone wanted to hold him. This one precious life was the hope and joy that we all needed.

HUMANITY

I think people are hardwired to connect. Our collective humanity is filled by giving love, sharing positive energy and practicing gratitude. I felt part of the beautiful cycle of giving and receiving—expanding our hearts and our capacity to give more. It was clear to me that kindness was percolating to the surface in powerful and wonderful ways in this time of great uncertainty and tragedy.

At a time of deep grief, terror and unresolved loss, to experience life-altering joy seems perverse. Maybe it was a microcosm of humanity—some grieve, some rejoice, some sigh with relief, some are found, some are lost, some will know, some will never know, some remember, some wish they could forget. While some are experiencing unimaginable pain, some are feeling deep gratitude for all that is happening.

In those moments, I was at the centre of humanity. As my son was born, many people died; some celebrated, while others mourned. Every person and every moment seemed to lie at the convergence of joy and grief, fear and contentment. That day, I found myself at the luckiest intersection of humanity. Grateful. Fully aware.

PRESENCE

I have learned that the magic of being Joe's mom exists in the space between. The space between confidence and self-consciousness, the space between what I think is right and what I believe is wrong, the space between worry and unquestionable knowing, the space between what makes me fearful and what is unrivalled joy, the space between what is painful and what takes your breath away. In the space between, beautiful memories are created—watching Joe lap up a story before he had words, hearing his infectious belly laughs, watching him throw his head back while I pushed him on a swing, inhaling and exhaling the whole world, seeing him walk into school the first time with a tiny backpack and huge courage. For certain, many of the beautiful memories are the classics like him losing his first tooth or his birthday parties, recitals or plays, but more often, they are the unscheduled, spontaneous, unpredictable precious moments.

In the space between, time stands still.
It allows us to stand solidly in each moment.
To hold space to breathe it all in.
In the space between, there are no regrets about the past and no worries about the future.

I Am Found

LESLEY ANN FARIA ADAMO

I want to tell you everything I know,
carry you and guide you.
Yet somehow, as your tiny finger points to
things in wonder and your eyes meet mine,
the paradigm shifts,
I once thought I was to show you the world.
When all along you came to show me.

Jessica Urlichs

I want to tell you everything I know, carry you and guide you

June 8th, 2017.
12:25 am
I am mama
I am mama
I am mama

I repeated these words to myself as I stared down at my newborn baby girl. I am mama, I declared. With equal calm and intensity, she stared up at me and our eyes locked. Time stood still, and the chaos of the room slipped away. The doctors, nurses, and family members seemed to disappear, and twenty-seven hours later, it was just us. Her gaze didn't leave mine for what felt like an eternity. Her eyes looked through me and told a story. A story that pointed to me as her North Star; her mama, her home. A story that had been thirty-two years in the making. I may have been her North Star, but at that moment, she had instantly become mine.

Without hesitation or reason, I knew that she had been what I had always been searching for. The girl who was forever at odds with herself had finally found her way home. Here, at this moment, I was home.

A duplicity lies in me that I have always known. A living embodiment of duality and contradiction; a polarization even. *Who am I? Who do I want to be? What do I stand for? How do I want to be perceived, and what will people think of me? What legacy will I leave behind?* These questions have, in many ways, guided and haunted me for the better part of my life. I was forever trying to pinpoint the answers, forever searching, forever questioning. Decisions made, opportunities lost, all in the vein of finding myself and discovering my higher calling and life's purpose.

It wasn't until giving birth to my daughter that light was shed on the questions that had forever swirled throughout my mind. In that moment of childbirth, my sweet girl had allowed for and ushered in my *rebirth*. The stars had aligned that day, and in the early hours of that Thursday morning, my questions finally had some answers. An inner-clarity emerged in me. Becoming mama was exactly *who* and *what* I was supposed to be. The stillness in my mind, the calm that came over me, the innate sense of all-knowing; all pointed in the same direction; being a mama was who I was. She had brought me home to myself.

I am mama. I thought with more conviction and certainty than I had ever felt before. This moment here; had changed me forever. My mind quieted—my vision and purpose clearer than they had ever been. *I was made to nurture,* I thought. I knew this instantly, deeply and whole-heartedly. I had long awaited for an accomplishment to fill me; a talent or even an adult relationship. I deeply believed that so much of my self-worth was rooted in my "doing". *What will I accomplish? How will I get there? How far can I push myself? How can I make the people I love proud or happy?* These questions became the framework for my life. They guided me. They rooted me. And ultimately, they pushed me. Forever pushing me forward in search of something greater than myself. This self-imposed pressure often served me well. It hadn't always felt crippling or like a burden that I had to carry. There were days and even years where this inner drive propelled me into great success and personal satisfaction. I was, and still am, a very driven person by nature. Always striving for more, constantly pushing myself to grow, achieve, and please.

The contradiction here lies in that at my core; I yearn for stillness. For calm. For peace. For quiet. For the first time in my life, the hustle of doing and going didn't define me, nor did it matter. In becoming mama I was finally given permission to just be.

Be present in the moment
Be her mama
Be me

She didn't need or want me to be anything other than that. No facade or expectations. No impressing or living up to the impossible standards that I had created for myself. For the first time in thirty-two years, I just *was.*

Judgement released. Forgiveness granted.

Yet somehow, as your tiny finger points to things
in wonder and your eyes meet mine,
the paradigm shifts

Fast forward three and a half years, and this little girl has not only become my life partner but ultimately my life's big *"why."* This time has been a journey of not only our relationship as mother and daughter but also a journey of finding myself in the sacredness and purity of that bond. The freedom that our relationship allows me is like nothing I have ever experienced before. This may not be every mother's journey, but it has surely been mine. The deep-rooted connection and unconditional love fill me in more ways than anything else ever could. This little soul was the "thing" that I had spent the better part of thirty-two years searching for. She was sent to me. She had chosen me, and I her.

In many ways, I have often felt unseen or unheard by many people in my life and I have become exceptionally good at masking that. Forever rising to the occasion and being the person that other people need me to be. I adapt, morph and mold until I fit. Forever in search of sincerity; forever in search of worthiness, at times feeling let down. Frequently feeling unaccepted or unseen by the circles that I travelled in—always guarding myself and protecting the places within me that I didn't allow most people to see. Never really knowing why I felt this way or where this feeling of lack had stemmed from and what it was rooted in.

In hindsight and in the growth that I have experienced over the course of the last few years, I now realize that I had never really taken the time to get to know *myself.* I found myself in a serious relationship at a very young age. One that ran its course through high school and ended timely in the later years of university. In many ways, I short-changed myself. Through no one's fault but my own, I allowed this relationship to take centre-stage. It consumed my time, energy and influenced the decisions that I made—not allowing myself to fully experience my adolescence and the freedom that comes with it—missing out on the learning that only happens when you have the freedom to be alone, unattached and uncommitted. The freedom to experience and learn who you are without the pressures of being accountable to someone else. Taking chances and growing in independence and experiencing life on your own; making those "selfish" choices and necessary mistakes. Allowing myself the time to just be. I can see now how this had a ripple and lasting effect on the path that I have journeyed and on the woman that I have become.

From a very young age, I was putting the needs and wants of others ahead of my own. Those formative years should have been spent exploring my identity and learning, leaning into new experiences. This is where this inner conflict and duplicity began. If I'm honest with myself, I always knew deep down that I was going through the motions and was yearning for my own space to grow and experience life. I allowed other people's opinions to penetrate my journey, forever worrying about what people would think if I veered from the path that I had chosen and created for myself. Rarely pausing to ask myself what I really wanted, and in some ways; losing my voice in the process.

But with her, all of this fades away. She sees me. No need to shift, change or pretend. She allows me to just be. There is a sacredness in this permission that she has granted me. A proverbial deep breath that I have finally taken.

I am worthy.
I am enough.
I am complete.

Breathe deeply, Lesley. All you need is already within you.

I know this now. These words have become my mantra. She has shown me the way. This lesson did not come easy, nor was it meant to. It was a childhood and adolescence filled with moments of choice and moments of unknowing. Years of feeling uneasy about my journey and path. It was a journey home to myself, to who I was called to be. Becoming mama ushered in more growth and space than I have ever known and put the pieces of me together in the most beautiful way. Shining a light on who I am at my core. In this role, I am enough, and I am worthy. I have surrendered and stepped into myself. Giving myself permission to let go of my judgements of who I think I'm supposed to be.

On the day before New Year's Eve 2020, I found myself standing in the shower, a stream of tears flowing down my face. Not fully knowing why, but knowing that I deeply needed this release. A release to help me let go of the past, a release to let me embrace the new. This past year has undoubtedly been a difficult one, not only as a collective but for me in personal ways as well. As I stood in the shower that night, the water clearing my thoughts, I could see so vividly that I had finally found a way to let go of the hold that other people had on me. I no longer felt a need to impress or change people's perceptions. *I am who I am*, I thought with newfound confidence. I finally know who I am, and I happen to really like her. What other people think of me is *not* my business. This was and still is a massive shift for me. I have always cared; always tried to change or fit in. It has been a lifetime in the making, but I now make myself a priority and realize the value in this. I assure myself daily that I am worthy, loved and deserving of being seen and heard. How can I lead my daughter on a journey of authenticity and self-love if I don't emulate this for her? I want to be a mirror for her as she is for me. Strong, confident, calm, radiating love and passion always.

I do not wish to pretend that these early years or days of becoming mama have always been seamless or easy; they absolutely have not been. Like everything else in this life that's worth having or doing, there have been the highest highs, but also many low lows. Growth is never without pain. It is in the pain that we see the brightness of the good and the expansion that is possible in all things. She was sent to usher in this change for me, to shift me and refocus my energy. I have chosen to surrender to the journey. She has become my mirror and has shown me who I was meant to live this life as. She is and will always be my driving force for growth. Through her, I am better, I am whole, I am me. I am forever growing as a person and as her mama.

My little person is now three and a half and acts as my mirror every single day. She shows up for me as I need her. She challenges, accepts, pushes and loves me so purely; in a way, I have never known. In our bond, I find what I am capable of. I see and hear the strength that lives within me. She pulls this from me and allows me to clearly see who I am at my most authentic. The strength, frustration, chaos and challenges that each day brings are balanced with sheer bliss, unconditional love and the purest sense of all-knowing and inner peace that I have ever known.

I once thought I was to show you the world,
when all along you came to show me

As I continue on this journey of life, I find myself better equipped than ever before. I now recognize that my intense need for change and the duality that lives in me; is me. I know now that it will forever be there and contribute to who I am and the decisions that I make. When the contradictions feel like a heavy burden to carry, I now have a safe place to fall. A safe place to be. I have learned that the beauty of me lies in this and flourishes here. I am complicated, full of potential, love, growth and duality. With the birth of my daughter came my life's greatest gift; *she has gifted me myself.* I know who I am now through her. She has shown me the way. This role and our relationship have guided me home. In her eyes, I see the best version of me. I see myself whole and complete, solid and unwavering. No longer in search, no longer yearning. This habitual mentality would always leave me in a state of lack because I wasn't meant to find my joy or purpose in my success or accomplishments. It never felt like it was enough, and that's because it just wasn't.

I have learned that it is not always in our doing or achieving that we feel complete or defined as a person. It is not always in our doing that we find our *way* or our *why.* Sometimes, it's the people that we love that will change us. No one has changed me more than my Ava.

We will journey together as partners. Undoubtedly pushing one another, and with certainty, we'll see our share of ups and downs. Highs and lows. We will drive each other crazy, fight and push one another to our brinks. No relationship is perfect. But, she has fulfilled me perfectly. I know with a beautiful sense of all-knowing and assurance; that no matter where this journey of life takes us, we will see each other through. I will forever guide her as she needs me to. Following her cues and allowing her to stand on her own, knowing that her mama will always stand by her no matter where her journey takes her. She will know with strong conviction that I will be there to catch her when she falls and when she is too scared to fly, to give her the strength she needs to see herself through. Feeling so unconditionally loved that she knows that she always has a cushion to fall on and that there will forever be someone out there who believes in her with the most unwavering love.

Above all, I yearn to imprint so much love on her that she will never feel the need to morph, change or seek acceptance from anyone but herself. Knowing that all she needs is already within her. In turn, my sweet girl will unknowingly do this for me just by being her, and just by being there. She will continue to remind me of my value, my worth and my life's purpose. It's her. It's us. It's what we are when we are together. Forever connected; perfectly imperfect.

I may never fully understand why it took becoming a mother to feel like I had finally become myself. This may always remain a beautiful mystery in more ways than one. I realize it may just be the way that my life has fallen into alignment. Part of the satisfaction here lies in the mystery of it all, in the unknowing and in the continued growth. Only now, instead of spending my life searching and worrying, I know that I have my little guide to light the way. To push me forward and to be my constant reminder of why I'm here and what I am capable of. She is my why. Her presence and love will see me through.

As they say, "the days are long, but the years are short." I remind myself of this constantly. Knowing full well that one day she will shift and grow in her own direction and journey, and in a way, away from me. She has allowed for the space to be present, teaching me that those are the only moments that really matter. The lessons that I have learned from her will remain with me always. She will forever be the little girl who brought her mama back home to herself.

I now insist on only looking ahead and moving forward with an open heart filled with gratitude and love. Gratitude for the life I have created and for the people who have always seen me through. I am hopeful, excited and at peace with the person I am and the person I am choosing to become. I am better equipped than ever before. The lessons I have learned will carry me forward into opportunities of growth and moments of expansion. For the first time in forever, I am fully leaning in with open arms and surrendering to what lies ahead. For the first time in forever, I am free.

I am mama

I am mama

I am mama

I am found.

Mothering Through Self-Empowerment

RUTH SCHALKHAUSER TOWER

The gnawing pit in my stomach and the heaviness in my heart signaled the all-consuming thought that I couldn't escape: I had failed as a parent.

I had been dreading this day for weeks, and even though I knew it was the right decision, I was about to change my kids' lives forever.

THE PERFECT RECIPE

I had always wanted to be a mom and create an amazing, loving family, much like the one I had been blessed to be born into. Growing up, I assumed my friends experienced the same unconditional love and support my parents showered upon me and my younger brother. I found out later how truly fortunate I was not to have bickering parents who fought all the time and to know that I'd be loved no matter how badly I might mess up (I surely put that to the test in my high school years). We did not have any real family drama (the only drama we experienced was much like that of the Brady Bunch), and family dinners and family game nights were the norm. But most of all, we had parents who remained happily married.

That, to me, is exceptional, and it was, in my opinion, the recipe for the perfect family.

Wanting to create that for my kids, I poured every bit of myself into being the best mom and wife possible. This was my purpose, it felt like what I was groomed for, and I took these roles on wholeheartedly. I was willing to overlook the fact that I had to let go of some of my other dreams (I wanted to get my PhD and teach as a college professor). And that I let go of pieces of myself in order to make my marriage work (being the subservient wife never felt right). Sacrificing for the sake of my children and our family did feel noble and right. My mom was my role model, and if she could sacrifice for the sake of the family, like forgoing a much needed new winter coat to provide for the pair of Gloria Vanderbilt jeans that I desperately needed (yes, needed!), then I could overlook the things I had to let go of in order to fulfill my dream.

I loved being the caregiver for my kids and meeting their needs, and before I knew it, I had naturally fallen into the rhythm of having all my time consumed with meeting everyone else's needs. Purpose and identity blended seamlessly together in the role of wife and mom, and with all of myself invested, the perfectionist in me was driven to excel in these roles. The downside of pouring yourself out so completely is that you eventually need to feel validated by others to feel worthy. And those moments of joy and fulfillment that you treasure become scattered around many more feelings of being spent, drained, and at times resentful that so many of the responsibilities land on you. All of that should have been a red flag, but I disregarded it because I followed the recipe, giving my children the foundation of a loving family that was together, whole, and giving them the best opportunities to grow and thrive.

Isn't it remarkable how we'll create a story in our minds about how something, like motherhood, should be, look like, feel like, and we'll do whatever it takes to live that out—even if it means sacrificing ourselves in the process? It's a great risk. Because what happens should it all start to fall apart? What does that say about us?

THE FAILING

I was now finding out because fast forward almost 20 years into my marriage, my two beautiful, trusting children, now 14 and 10, were seated in front of me and my husband in the home that we had built as we delivered the news that we were getting divorced. The path that led us to this point is a story for another time, although the parts that matter here are the fact that after 20 years, I ended up feeling unfulfilled, unhappy in my marriage, and so disconnected from myself that I struggled even to make simple decisions based on what I wanted. This is where years of putting others ahead of myself had led me. I felt like an empty shell with resentment seeping into the cracks, my heart small and tight, except in this moment, it felt like it would burst out of my chest.

It didn't matter how well I told the story to my children that it wasn't their fault, that the things that mattered most wouldn't change, that they'd still be loved and nurtured—the world as they knew it was changing. I could feel the ground being torn apart beneath them. I saw the uncertainty in their eyes and sensed their knowing of betrayal, or maybe that was my own projection. But there was no denying the knowing, deep within me, that I had failed at the very thing that mattered most to me.

Woven into that moment of heartbreak was a small thought nagging at the back of my mind that wouldn't go away. It was actually a thought that had tried to surface on many occasions, only to be reburied each time: *I wanted more*. I don't think at the time I realized what that truly meant. But there was a feeling, one that brought with it immense guilt, that I wanted to do more with my life than just raise my kids and create an amazing family. And maybe the divorce would provide me with the opportunity to start over and figure that out. To even acknowledge that thought at that moment deepened the pit in my stomach and tugged at my heart. The guilt that came with it weighed heavily, because this idea flew in direct opposition to all I believed, to the story I had created for myself.

REMAKING CAROL BRADY

The story of what it meant to be a good, nurturing mom had been passed down to me through generations and society. It wasn't just in the selfless way I saw it lived out how my mom cared for me and my brother. My grandmother had her own inspiring story of overcoming challenges (my grandfather was an alcoholic who eventually got sober), and being a pillar of strength, sacrifice, and service for her family. I grew up watching Ma Ingalls on the TV show "Little House on the Prairie," be sacrificial, steadfast, and have a singular purpose, giving everything for her family. And Carol Brady from the Brady Bunch (I watched this show every day when I got home from school) sent the message to me, even through humor, how important it was to be the glue that held her family together.

Sure the feminist movement was in full force, giving women permission to do more than just raise their kids. We could also have a career, but it was still done with the energy of "I can bring home the bacon, fry it up in a pan, and never ever let you forget you're a man." Us women, we do it all, hold it all together, work hard, sacrifice—and it's all worth it. I heard that message loud and clear and, over the years, added, "and then I'll be worthy."

These were the stories and ideas that shaped my own, the ones that had been driving me and I had been striving to live out. And I had failed.

It would take a while before I picked up the shattered pieces and would put them back together in a much more empowering way for myself. At first, I continued the role of mother as I knew it because I thought that would support my children the best. As heartbreakingly challenging as the decision to get divorced was, in retrospect, it was the best thing that could have happened to me and my kids. Hindsight never fails to deliver much-needed perspective. And hitting rock bottom was the impetus I needed to rewrite the story in a much more empowering way.

REWRITING THE SCRIPT

I came to eventually understand that I hadn't failed. The story and identity that I had been trying so hard to live out is what had failed. It was never my truth. It never totally resonated with how I felt. It denied me the ability to be my true self because I constantly left myself out of the equation. That was a liberating realization. I was moving from mothering through sacrifice to mothering through empowerment, starting with myself.

As I began to put together my new life post-divorce, I took apart all of the stories and put myself back in the role of the leading lady of my life, which meant I had to write a new definition of how I would mother. I did this somewhat consciously, but years later, I can see more clearly the wisdom of the path I was creating for myself and my children. I would be the mom who loved and cared for her kids, but I would no longer live for them. Of course, this didn't mean that I loved them any less or even that they were any less important. This was a mindset shift that put me back in the circle of what was important, and just like I didn't want to let them down, I was no longer willing to let myself down.

I started to believe in myself more and to honor my thoughts and ideas. That nagging feeling that I had about wanting more was about wanting to do more with my life, but it was also about wanting to be more of who I am. That meant not giving my power away by trying to please others or make them happy or need their validation. For years if someone wasn't happy, somehow it became my responsibility to fix it, or even worse, it was my fault. My happiness now was just as important as others. I would choose for me, which also allowed me to suddenly have stronger opinions, and I went from "whatever you want" to "I want to do this".

What I wanted to do was to take time for the things I loved to do—yoga, running, time with girlfriends, even getaways and retreats by myself—and so I did all of those things, and in the process, showed my kids how important it was to prioritize self-care. I purchased my first car all by myself, which at the time felt like a big gift of self-worth as I drove off the lot in my brand new Mini Cooper, sunroof open, music blaring, feeling free, and independent. And then, I took my passion for yoga, went through yoga teacher training, and started my own business. I opened a yoga studio. When someone at my Open House asked if I was the owner, saying "Yes" was a moment of self-ownership—I was an entrepreneur and owned my own studio! Following through on my desires wasn't just fulfilling; it had rebuilt my belief in myself and my worth.

I thought I empowered my kids by giving them every opportunity, by sacrificing so they could have more. In the process, they became my life, and my identity was wrapped up with them, and I lost my belief in myself. I couldn't raise empowered children if I didn't believe in myself. My own empowerment became the foundation for how I would nurture and care for my children. As a mom, I dismantled all the ideals and expectations I had for my kids so that they could discover their own. When I lived for my kids, it was so easy to fall into the trap of wanting to shape and mold my kids into who I thought they should be instead of allowing them to be who they were. After my shift in self-worth, I nurtured them by validating who they were, empowering them to own their feelings, take control of their thoughts, and claim their power to choose—all things I had needed to learn to do for myself first.

LEAVING A LEGACY

I can see now that what I started to do years ago, post-divorce, by rewriting my story by becoming self-empowered, was how I would begin to leave my kids a better legacy. Sure, the legacy that was passed down to me was a beautiful one. I wouldn't be where I am today were it not for the love, support, and example of my parents and grandparents. But when it became my turn to pass down a legacy, my story needed to shift.

I believe that my children see in me what is possible for their lives if they do the same thing and own the narrative of their story. And to make sure that story fits exactly who they are. No more molding to fit something that isn't aligned with your highest truth. This now is a story of greater possibility. Of living a life of deep purpose and meaning. And yes, of creating a beautiful, loving family along the way. I am now remarried, and my husband and I have created a new family for the four of us.

A couple of years ago, my daughter wrote me the most thoughtful, beautiful birthday card (actually, all of her cards to me are like that!). Our relationship has grown dramatically in closeness over the years, which was an unexpected gift that rose from the ashes of the divorce as I became my true self. To witness this in her heartfelt expression, and see through her the legacy that I was now living and how my choices were affecting her, brought me to tears. Here's part of what she wrote:

> *"You are such an inspiration to me and everyone surrounding you—you bring endless life, love, and good energy everywhere you go. I hope you know how loved and cherished you are, and that you have improved the lives of so many people simply by being you. Your life story inspires me daily, especially what you do now to help so many women. You have such an incredible strength that they all need, and the characteristics that make you such a wonderful teacher and role model. I say all this on behalf of them because I don't think you get enough credit for all the amazing things you do in your life, or for how far you've come and how much you've grown. I see it now even compared to when I was young, which is why I admire you so much. You are my best friend, my #goals, the person I tell everything to, the one I count on for advice, the wonderful woman who I hope to grow up to embody."*

Each of our lives leaves a legacy; they tell a story in one way or another. As a mother, I believe my job is to live my story in the most empowering way by living as my true self and living out my purpose. Only then can I guide my children to do the same. I mother and nurture my children through self-empowerment. First mine, then theirs. Each time I choose in favor of myself, I strengthen the relationship with myself, my power, and my inner knowing, which makes me like a super mom because I'm now better able to meet my kids' needs.

There is something deep within each of us that longs to be fulfilled. It doesn't happen by following the conventional norms or roles or even the stories and expectations handed down to us. Whether we realize it or not, we all have stories beneath the surface running our thoughts and actions. These stories need to be questioned, examined, and ultimately healed. And when we begin to own and rewrite the story of who we truly are, when we live as our true selves, that is when we mother through empowerment and create an incredible legacy for our children and generations to come.

The Strength Within

EDEN PEREIRA

Take a minute and remember how you felt when your pregnancy test read positive. When you saw that faint second line appearing, questioned if it was real, and still decided to redo the test to be one-hundred-percent certain. When the Doctor told you that you were pregnant, how did you feel? Were you excited, scared, nervous, proud?

You remember that feeling of knowing you were pregnant. Your closest friends forewarned and spoke to you about how your body would feel different, especially your breasts, and that your instincts would just know. You're anxious for your partner to leave because you want to do it alone. Even though you know you're excited, deep down, you're scared because you have no idea what your pregnancy journey will be like.

It has finally sunk in that you are pregnant. You took one test, and two very faint lines appeared. You paced back and forth, took a picture and sent it to two close friends. You needed to be certain, so you go out and get another test. The longest three-minute wait of your life, but there it was, in dark block letters, the word PREGNANT. You're so excited that you want to scream it to the whole world and tell everyone the amazing news. First things first, your partner, he is overjoyed, even though you didn't do it with him there, but he knew you were pregnant earlier in the week. You want to see him and celebrate, but you already had a session booked, so you go out to get some t-shirts made. You want your families to be the first to know.

How will they take it? How will your partner's family react? Am I ready for this?

We head to tell the future Abuelo and Abuela that they are going to be grandparents. We had the perfect plan, you love surprising people, which was an occasion for something memorable. You had your sweater zipped up, and your partner went to change his shirt. His sister's mouth dropped, and we quickly told her it was a surprise. He walked over to his mom and aunt, nothing; no one noticed that he changed his shirt from light to dark. Then finally, his aunt realizes, "Que no!" nudges to her sister, "Read!" It takes her a second to read her son's shirt; they embrace with tears of joy in their eyes. His dad and uncle walk into the room confused, "Que passo?" They read his shirt, and the love that filled the room was indescribable.

You are going to be a Mom!

The next day you get to your Mom's house. You feel like you're going to throw up before you even get in the door. It was certainly the nerves and not morning sickness. You want the moment to be perfect, and you continue to exchange looks with your partner because the nerves and excitement are just too much to feel. Lunchtime is over, and you tell your sister you got her something; as she opens the bag, you unzip your sweater and start to cry, "NO!" Your Mom says, and all you do is cry. "I knew it!" screams your sister. The whole room is filled with tears of love and so much joy.

You are going to be a Mom!

You go to bed after a weekend of pure joy. You reflect on the adventure that is coming. You pray that you will be half the Mother your Mom has been to you. You have always admired your mother's strength because you saw the struggle and heartache she went through at a young age. From raising three beautiful girls all on her own in Canada to chasing what she thought was her soulmate to a country where she had no helping hands. To have her whole world ripped out from under her and move back to Canada, alone, with the only thing keeping her going being your sisters and you. You saw her tirelessly working three-to-four jobs just to keep a roof over your head and food on the table. Whatever means necessary, she shaped life for you. She taught you how to be the best role model, a Mother, without you even knowing.

You are ready to take this head-on. You smile so big; you cry as you touch your belly.

You are going to be a Mom!

Everything begins to change as there are many things you need to do to get ready for this bundle of joy. There is so much you need to prepare yourself for. You need to make sure you are healthy. You need to know that you had the best Mom in the world, who has taught you all you need to know. It's okay to be scared, but know you are not on this journey alone.

Deep down, you think of all that can go wrong. You want to do your very best to protect yourself and your baby.

You have your first appointment with your Doctor. Excitement was felt as you entered the office. The Doctor comes in. She simply tells you that you need to start taking prenatal vitamins and tells you how important it is to take them daily, "See you in four weeks."

"Wait, what? Don't I need to get bloodwork or an ultrasound to confirm?" you asked. She replies, "No, you did two tests, and your period is regular, right?"

Shouldn't this be a big deal? She hasn't seen me in years. You just need to know that there truly is a baby growing inside of you.

Will I ever feel that connection?

Everyone you speak to talks about the connection they had with their babies while they grew in the womb. You constantly ask yourself, if you will have that connection?

When does it happen? Will my child even love me?

Weeks pass, and you finally get the confirmation that your human chorionic gonadotropin (HCG) levels are good. HCG is a hormone usually produced by the placenta. You still feel nothing, no connection, no movement, but your body is showing slight changes. You have longed for this time, but you also thought it would be so different.

For weeks you long to feel a bond, even the flutters that everyone talks about, but still nothing. Your friends and family are so excited as they are constantly asking how you are feeling. Your fiance takes every night to cuddle with you and talk to your belly; little did he know it made you feel horrible because to you, there is nothing in there.

Why can't you just give me a sign?

You wake up on your first day in the second trimester, feeling normal. As you lay in bed, you try to talk to your baby in hopes you feel something. Emptiness fills you, and immediately you cannot control it but cry. "I'm sorry..." are the only words you can bear to say.

You continue to lay in your bed, finding the peace and strength to get up and get ready to go to work. You lay there just a little longer, and find yourself remembering back to when your Mom did it all on her own. Even your grandmother's strength is always shown through, until her last breath. She cared for you just as much as your Mother did; she was your protector when your Mother wasn't there. It didn't matter how busy or how sick she was; she always made the effort to be there. You had always wanted her to be there when you became a Mother, and you know that she gave you little signs that she was proud of you. Even though becoming a Mother is a little different, you know that being strong will get you through this.

One morning you wake up, touch your belly as you do every day, but today was different. You felt a bump... an ever so small bump. "Hello, my baby." You get so excited that you take a picture to remember that moment. You and your partner are so excited to meet your baby. For the first time, aside from the day you told your family, you felt the joy you wanted to feel when you're pregnant. It didn't last though, in your mind, you wondered and questioned everything. You wanted more than anything to feel a connection.

Will I ever be a great Mom like my mother?

You spend some time thinking about your relationship with your Mom. You have always admired the strength she had growing up. She has been your superwoman for most of your life, and now it's your turn to be someone else's superwoman. You're terrified because, in the back of your mind, you grew up without a father. You are afraid that one day you will be on your own too, so your instincts try to control everything. This journey will not be like any you have been through. You know your partner is behind you through it all. You found yourself battling your emotions and your past more often than not.

Think back to when you were a child. Did your Mom ever seem out of alignment, upset, or scared? She found strength each day in you and your siblings. You kept her going, regardless of the amount of time she spent with you all, you still knew she loved you.

She set the example that when times are tough, we find strength in what matters the most. We find strength through our children.

Week eighteen's Anatomy Scan is quickly approaching and what would be your only ultrasound, as your Doctor said. Your only instructions were to drink many fluids, and to not go to the washroom. That was easier said than done. You are showing now but still just feels like you are bloated. You invite your sisters to come along because you need them to be a part of the journey. So many thoughts were running through your head.

Will your baby be healthy? How many are you having? Will the technician ruin the surprise and tell you what the sex of the baby will be?

It was a surreal moment. Holding your fiance's hand ever so tight, you observe the room and see the smiles on your sisters' faces—just pure love in that tiny room. We specifically say we would like to leave the sex as a surprise and to please only let my sisters know.

We were able to see our baby's head, legs, hands and spine. *This baby is mine*, was the first thought that came to my mind. You helped create a tiny human who will call you Mama, Mom, Mommy one day. A massive wave of emotions fills your body, and you just want that feeling to stay forever.

"Would you like to hear the heartbeat?" No words were spoken, just smiles and tears of joy. A healthy heartbeat was beating ever so quickly—the heartbeat of a baby that I hope to make proud one day. You quickly close your eyes to cherish this moment to put into your memory bank, your subconscious mind, to remember during your moments of fear and doubt. This moment is a piece of strength to keep you going, a reminder that you will be a Mother!

My baby, please, can you give Mommy a sign?

A few weeks after your anatomy scan, you're at the mall and starting to feel pregnant more and more each day, walking around window shopping with your fiance and his family. You're in the middle of a conversation with your sister-in-law, mid-sentence and bam; you feel something that makes you stop in your tracks. Your sister-in-law asks you if you're okay. You continue walking a little further, still talking, bam again, "Ow!" "Are you sure you're okay?" she asks, a little worried now. "Um, yeah, I think I just need to sit down." Everyone is now a little concerned as you sit there, not saying anything. You just continue to stare down and rub your belly. "The baby kicked, I just felt the first real kick, something." You hold your belly with such pride for a moment. You felt your baby, as you have been asking for something, and finally, they gave you just that! You start to think, *was this what strength entailed?* Going about each day as usual and trusting the process? Could this all just be in my head because I wanted a sign so badly? Yes, your body is changing, but surely there had to be more to just feeling bloated? I will be a Mom soon; there needs to be more.

A few more weeks pass, and we plan a Gender Reveal party for our closest family and friends. It turned out to be the hottest day of the summer. Our siblings were so excited and planned out the day, something nice and casual. We chose 2:45 pm for the reveal to ensure everyone important could be there. You thought you were having a girl for the longest time; secretly you wanted a girl, but so did your partner. It was time everyone chose a side, Team Girl to our right and Team Boy to our left. The countdown started... 10, 9, 8...

you could hear all the screaming, GIRL! BOY!... 7, 6, 5... this was it, you find out if the baby will be a male or female... 4, 3, 2... you just remember closing your eyes for a quick second with all the nerves, you don't want to look... 1!!!! Your fiance kicks the plastic soccer ball... BLUE dust flies everywhere. You scream and start to cry as you hug your partner.

Santiago, you are going to be so loved, my precious baby boy. This was all you could think about. Time stopped at that very moment.

You're going to be a Mom, to a boy!

Everyone circled us to congratulate you, and some, "I told you!" and "I knew it!" were the words swirling all around us. At that moment, it was the first true moment it felt real.

Your whole journey has now changed. Your baby boy will be here before you know it, so many things to prepare. This has been a challenging ride for you, but you begin to see that this all happened to take the steps you were supposed to feel in your pregnancy. You were meant to feel alone to remind you of your past and who you strived to be better for. You needed to take the time to feel the connection with your son to symbolize the journey your Mom went on and allow yourself to remember that through everything, these moments are the ones you need to be fully present for. The constant thing you had in this journey was strength, trust and love.

As a human being, you always feel the need to be in control, know the steps before they happen, but this time there was no manual. You needed to allow yourself to feel and build your strength as a Mother. You were tested time and time again because you now see the true value of a woman bearing a child for nine long months. Your connection begins through strength and, in turn, creating that indescribable bond with your child.

What has your journey to becoming a Mother taught you?

Your journey is your own, but you are not alone. Do not be hard on yourself; allow your partner in. Share this journey with them because you will grow stronger together.

Allow yourself to feel all the emotions. Reminisce of your past, the good, bad, happy and the ugly. It will give you some comfort in knowing the type of Mother you'd like to be for your child. This is the perfect time to also allow yourself to forgive those people or relationships that need it. Entering Motherhood strong will allow you to be the perfect role model and pave the way for your child.

Give yourself time to process the journey you are on. Embrace the changes your body is going through. As a woman, we endure the most pain but the best joy. Give yourself time to admire the growth of your belly. Some women dream for this time and then take it for granted. One thing you will cherish is just sitting or laying and admiring the bump, the kicks, the movement and the hiccups. Soak it all in, Mama!

Where can you find strength in your journey to being a Mother?

More Than a Mother

STEFANIA TERSIGNI

MY UNIVERSE BLEW OPEN

If I told you becoming a mother was hard for me, I'd be lying. Getting pregnant was the easy part. My husband and I couldn't believe it happened so quickly that we actually decided that he would take a pregnancy test to see what a negative test looked like! I still laugh at that story; both of us sitting on the bathroom floor waiting for the negative pregnancy test results. Seriously though, I LOVED being pregnant. I often catch myself saying that if I could find a way to bottle up how I felt during my pregnancies, I would drink that potion every day! I was healthy, glowing, radiant, sensual and literally full of life. When that magical time arrived, and I held my newborn son close to my heart, my whole universe blew open! Becoming a mom is when my world lit up with purpose. At that moment, I stepped into my power. This chapter is a glimpse into my motherhood journey, but more than that, it is the journey of being a mother that brought me closer to my life's purpose and taught me self-love. I am a mother, but I am also the creator of my inner world and life experiences, and you can be too.

Being an awesome mom without losing yourself in all its responsibilities and expectations is challenging. On this one particular afternoon, I was working on this chapter at my kitchen table while also arranging how my son was going to get to his hockey practice. I was also planning dinner, avoiding folding laundry, marking my students' tests, scheduling my dog's walk, and getting distracted by emails. In addition, my daughter was staring me down as she patiently waited for me to paint her nails. Notice that I didn't even mention my husband yet? God bless him. On most days, he's at the end of the line. He'll have his moment in this chapter. After all, it's partly because of him that we have our babies.

THE MOTHER FIGURE VS. SELF LOVE

When I reflect on the mother figures in my life, I see admirable women who selflessly give their love to their families, oftentimes at the price of sacrificing their own needs and desires. This is where I found myself caught at a crossroads. I have this deep love and respect for these principal women, but at the same time, I knew I couldn't and wouldn't let that happen to me. That style of nurturing didn't resonate with the mother I envisioned myself to be. *Could one still love so deeply while not having to sacrifice herself at the same time?* The "idea" of motherhood and how it looked in the past versus what I thought I was supposed to do and be could easily take over my whole identity. I wasn't enthusiastic about giving that up. There had to be a better way—a way where I could love so fiercely while not surrendering my true self.

We often hear the words '*self-love*' floating around, and it's the realization of these beautiful, simple and powerful words that flipped the switch on motherhood for me. How could I show my children the true meaning of love if I didn't show them that loving ourselves is part of it too? In becoming a mother and raising my children, I was presented with a sacred space to come home to myself. The true me didn't have to be lost. I admit, at times, I found myself a victim of social and self-inflicted pressures of motherhood, but I would be found again and again because I loved myself so deeply. I have my son and daughter to thank for that beautiful reminder every day.

CLARITY IN THE CHAOS

Call it 'mommy brain', brain fog or simply part of the aging process, but I don't remember much about my life before my babies. Obviously, I had a life, but few details seem to hold much substance now that I have my children. I often ask myself, what was I REALLY doing before I had my kids? I had my children, and suddenly I found clarity in the chaos of motherhood. I found my sacred circle—my life partner, my children and myself. My husband and I had laid the foundation for the life we wanted to live. Our children are beautiful extensions of that. They are the extensions of who we are as a family but also their own entities. Once I surrendered to that idea, life around me seemed to refocus. I became more present. I chose to live and act with more intention. I knew who I wanted to be and who I didn't want to be—not only for myself but, more importantly, for my children.

When you allow yourself to transform your inner world and step into your power, you give others permission to do the same. I'd like to help you do that for yourself if you'll allow me. You can always revisit this part in this chapter when you're ready to try this visualization. Gift yourself the time to carve out this space and be committed to this self-love practice. If you're ready now, let's begin.

Take this moment to become present.
Inhale...
Fill up and take in what you need...
Exhale...
Release what no longer serves you ....
Soften your shoulders, jaw and brows...
Lean and settle into yourself...
Begin to visualize your Highest Self... How does she look?... How does she present herself?...
Sit with her... Feel her energy... Take in her surroundings...
What dialogue is being shared?... What message does she have for you?... Listen...
Reach out your arms and embrace her... Feel her divine energy and power being transferred to you...

When you're ready to release her, bring the palm
of your hands to your heart... Smile, knowing your
Highest Self is always there..... Hold onto this
precious moment as long as you need...
Inhale...
Fill up and take in what you need...
Exhale...
Release what no longer serves you ....
When you're ready, gently return to your space.

How do you feel now? Take this time to scan your physical, emotional, mental and even spiritual body. Maybe find a piece of paper and pen to jot down or even sketch your experience.

Know you can come back to this cherished moment and revisit your Highest Self whenever you feel you have lost touch with her. Remember, this power is always within you. Let your Highest Self be your guide in motherhood and life.

A DIFFERENT PERSPECTIVE

There is another important and influential person in my life: the father of my children. My high school sweetheart, first love, life partner and best friend. I told you he'd make a comeback, but I warn you, you may have mixed feelings about what I'm going to tell you next. He once confessed to me that he put me—his wife—before our kids. You're probably wondering how he could say that? You can hate him; I certainly felt that emotion. However, as you read on, you will understand his intentions for saying those words to me.

When he made that statement, our kids were under four years old and all-consuming as toddlers should be. Straight up, his words broke my heart. I believed as parents, our children came before us—as wife and husband. Even though his words would haunt me now and then, I decided to let it go and not make a big deal of it. As the years passed and our toddlers turned into teenagers, my husband's words came back to me and started to take on a different meaning. I found myself with more time on my hands as my children became more independent. This was when I realized it was just as important for my son and daughter to see their mom (and dad) as human beings with their own interests and passions.

It was my husband's words that challenged me to look beyond my life as a mom. As much as I love motherhood and consider it my most important vocation ever, it became clearer to me that I needed to start making time for personal exploration, learning and growth. Today, I can perceive what my husband's message truly meant: not to forget who I am. To not forget who we are to each other as lovers and partners in life; to not lose myself in being a mom when I am so much more!

The reality is that my kids are growing up, and they don't need me every second of the day. I have to seek them out most of the time. As much as it makes my eyes water and tears away at my heart, I know they will one day leave our cozy nest and journey along their own path to discovering their life's purpose. Ultimately, isn't this what I want for them? Yes, there is no doubt. My children, grown-up, independent and self-sufficient. I prefer not to think that far, but when that happens, and when the kids are grown up, living their lives, who will be left? You guessed it—my husband and I. Just us two. And that's what the father of my children and my partner in life meant about putting me first. He is, in fact, putting us first.

I AM LOVING AWARENESS

In the chaos of figuring out how I could be the mom I vowed to be, I had to unlearn what many generations before me had lived. Putting motherhood aside for a moment, I personally asked, "*What is my identity and all the things that make me—me?*" Thus began the journey of the Self. I took the leap, and with the support of my husband and children, I decided to work part-time as a school teacher and immerse myself in yoga teacher training, meditation, life coaching, and reiki. During this period, I connected closely with the concept of Mother Earth—the ultimate nurturer and provider of all who selflessly gives herself to all. I found comfort in the fact that "nature doesn't rush and yet all is accomplished." (-Lao Tzu) There blossomed my new personal mantra: *I am loving awareness.*

Along my journey, I looked closely at the concepts of the 'Self'. Curious and sometimes in turmoil over trying to define who I was, I found comfort and answers in my yoga and meditation practice. Here, I learned more about the 'Ego' and the 'True Self'. The Ego, also known as the false self, is dependent on everything we have learned from our environment and experiences. Often we turn to our superficial self as a means of daily protection from situations and ultimately survival. As a mother, it is easy to get caught up in parenting from the Ego Self. We are, in fact, mama bears protecting our cubs. I intentionally make an effort not to parent from the Ego Self. It's challenging, and I don't always succeed, but when I can quiet my mind and simply observe the space, people, and situation—I can allow myself to parent from my True Self. I am a present and mindful parent. *I am loving awareness.* I parent from a place that reflects my core values and true essence of being. *I am loving awareness.* I am not the reactor but the seer and observer. *I am loving awareness.* I recognize I am not solely my experiences, my mistakes or even my triumphs. *I am loving awareness.* I choose to connect with my soul and recognize that everything and everyone has a soul. *I am loving awareness.* I set intentions to raise and support my children with the guidance and positive energy of my True Self. *I am loving awareness.*

THE FRUITS OF MY LABOUR

I am redefining what being a positive mother figure to my children looks like every day. It's challenging and exhausting work, but it's also the most rewarding undertaking of my life. I see my family, husband and children, as partners in my life. I am consciously aware and present of the nurturer I wish to be and the flourishing relationship I commit to creating with my kids. They're growing up, and in turn, our relationship is changing. I know I have to adapt to the dynamic nature that mothering and nurturing presents to me. I am open and excited to grow and evolve with my children.

We are a family united, but we are also separate entities living our own lives. We celebrate each other's victories, and we are there to support one another during challenging times. I choose to walk alongside my family, sometimes being the cheerleader on the sidelines, but always ensuring they know that I support their dreams, desires and the life path they choose.

As I encourage my children to explore all the possibilities and discover parts of themselves, I show them daily that I do the same. I am not only their 'busy' mom, mindlessly running around checking off items from my daily to-do list. I am their 'present' mom, revealing to them that they have the power to manifest and live the life they wish to live. As I learn from my kids and my experiences as a mom every day, I also learn more about myself and the energy I want to put out into the universe. More profoundly, the legacy I want to leave behind for my family becomes more vivid—one of love, hope, unity, compassion, strength and gratitude.

MOTHERHOOD: THE GIFT THAT KEEPS ON GIVING

If you're going to take anything away from this story about my motherhood journey, I hope it is that you recognize the importance of not only nurturing your children but also remembering to step into your unique power and nurture yourself too. I am by no means a 'mom expert', but I am a mother of two wonderful human beings. Even though I still have a lot to experience and learn along my motherhood journey, I do hold dear some valuable gems of advice that I freely share with any open and willing moms out there.

GEMS OF ADVICE

- *Be aware of the mother you want to be.* Recognize that the role models of the past may not resonate with your style of nurturing today.
- Which brings me to... *There is no 'one' definition or way of being a mother.* You may admire and also look to other mom figures for advice and support, but make it your own!

- *Be in the present moment as much as possible.* As a mom, it's natural to plan ahead and make sure everything is thought of and even cared for. Delegate some of that responsibility to your children. They will learn and be better for it. This way, you can live each day with intention.
- *Recognize that even though you gave your child life—that it is their life to live.* Be conscientious when you are getting too caught up in what they could be or what you want them to be. Cherish them for who they are today.
- *Be the best mom you can be on any given day.* Trust me, it will vary. Remember to give yourself permission to be gentle with yourself. Own and learn from your mistakes and, more importantly, celebrate your 'mom of the year' moments.
- *Empower yourself in self-love, self-nourishment and self-accomplishment outside of being a mom.* Discover or continue to nurture a hobby, craft, or skill. Continue to explore the things that bring joy and purpose to your life. Get in touch with your Higher Self and recognize what that means to your happiness.
- *Invite your children to experience the true you.* I am me with my kids—I don't lie, I don't hold things back, I follow my gut, and I speak my truth. I am human, I am real, I make mistakes, I get down

on myself, and most importantly, I get right back up and figure it out. In turn, I can only hope and encourage them to do the same with me.

- *Realize and honour that there is freedom in surrendering.* The Universe has your back. What is meant to be, will be. You don't need to control everything. It's physically impossible. What if you were open to all the possibilities that lie ahead? Give it a try. You may surprise yourself.

NOT THE END—ALWAYS A BEGINNING

I know the stars aligned for me the moment I became a mother. My first child was born, and I wanted to be everything for him. Shortly after, my daughter was born, and I counted my blessings for being gifted with not one but two beautiful and healthy children. I am grateful every day for this precious gift. I take this gift of motherhood seriously and also not-so-seriously. I intentionally choose to guide and support them, but I also surrender to what life may bring on its own. I plan ahead, but I also enjoy and cherish the moment for what it is. My children and husband have helped me become and love the person I am today; a mother and so much more. Together with the love I have for myself, they are my reason and always will be. The journey continues, and that brings with it much anticipation and excitement. Motherhood is bound to leave its mark, and I am proud to wear its scars and badges. My hopes are that you've been inspired to live each day in your true power as you become the mom and person you're meant to be. Your Higher Self is there—set her free!

Who You're Meant to Be

NICKI DI GRAVINA

LEVELS OF LOVE

The warmth of the sun comforts her as she lays on the grass, looking up at the sky. Taking it in, all at once—knowing that she's exactly where she's meant to be. The swirl of colour and sound and the grass beneath her. All of it, there for her in that very moment and for always. Open and eager to be alive with a sensitivity that she learned to believe was a weakness. Alba was just a girl with so much love in her heart, and deep down, she knew she was meant for more.

She knew that there was nothing like the levels of love that life had to offer. Her parents' love was the kind made for the movies when love letters were the only option, and commitment was a natural choice. They were perfectly imperfect, which made their love possible. Her grandparents' love was waiting for her with gentle and calm affection. From her grandfather's sweet greetings to the way her grandmother affectionately referred to Alba as her *Stella Polare* (North Star). All so different in many ways, yet their compassion is what connected them to her. In time she became an aunt, and whenever her family grew, so did her self-awareness. Each of them taught her what it meant to love from a place that is pure and unconditional. They were a part of her love story, uncovering a missing piece of her heart that she longed to fill with a deeper love, a mother's love.

Alba continued to take in the world with an intensity that overwhelmed her and became who she thought she should be. With excitement and anticipation of where life would take her, she learned to own her independence. She protected her heart and held onto who she was becoming. Then, an unexpected love came to her. An easy love, the kind that is comforting and passionate, understanding, and unwavering. Their unforgettable memories reassured her and gave her hope. He stood with her, and her with him by each other's side as their love became one that could endure everything in life.

She learned to self-nurture through the life moments that shaped her. Through the memories, the lessons and losses, the heartaches and disappointments, prepared her for who she was meant to be. The memories of her mother's recovery from a failing heart weeks before her wedding day abruptly put life into perspective. It was a lesson in letting go, and one she later learned would save her life. Alba was uncomfortable with facing the fragility of life but finally could see that her mother loved everyone more than she loved herself, which no longer served her. On her wedding day, she saw her mother's strength and determination, and the truth; that her mother did the best she could that day and all the days before. It was clear that sometimes even on our best days, it just may not be enough for everyone else, and that's ok.

And so, life went on with interruptions of struggle and possibility. The possibility of becoming a mother was when she knew it was *her* time, yet it wasn't. She struggled with disappointment which fed her fears as she ignored her instinct and betrayed herself. Convinced that she was to blame and undeserving, but deep inside, she could feel it somehow, that she was meant for that level of love—a mother's love. *Was she running out of time?* The pressure was building, tapping her on the shoulder at every turn. She was enveloped with reminders that her dreams were out of reach. Until she chose to let go and lean into the uncertainty and decided that *her* dreams take time.

HER TRUTH

Carrying a child was everything to her because it was as though she was becoming whole. The moment her baby was placed in her arms, she received her missing piece and a new life. She was discovering the levels of unconditional love that made sense of everything. It was all in preparation to meet new corners of her heart and soul. Her future had finally arrived. Her baby girl, the one that made her a mother, her dream come true. It was the beginning of losing herself in the joys that come with being a mother. Alba cherished every day with her, and it was their love that gave her permission to unlearn who she thought she should be, and it left her reaching for more. It was an extraordinary time, the in-between of having one child. She gained newfound confidence as the opportunities to grow were made available to her. She learned so much about herself, yet it didn't seem to prepare her for what life had in store for her.

She can recall the day she found out that she was expecting again. Alba could feel her body changing, and she recognized the familiar shifts with a new awareness. Taking her time while enjoying the moment when she confirmed what she already knew in her heart—that he was with her. It was a new and familiar experience. Challenging her and her body differently, dealing with so much, including the mommy guilt. Afraid that she wouldn't be able to love the same as she did with her first and that her little girl wouldn't know how much love mommy had to give. All of it weighed on her, but she survived the doubt, the fears, and the delivery. He arrived with determination—open and eager to be alive. Alba finally met her little one, the one she knew belonged to her and her to him. He was what she needed, guiding and teaching her new levels of love she didn't know she was capable of. Their family was complete, and she now could love them more.

The blurred memories of diapers, bottles, pre-school, and baths. The bedtime stories, sleepy-faced snuggles and the sweet sounds of their giggles. Exhausted and grateful, yet afraid that the ideal life she created in her mind had the undeniable power to sabotage her truth. The unreality she deeply wished for simply couldn't stand up to real life. The smallest expression and quiet moments that could easily have gone unnoticed is when Alba tried to ignore the whispers in her heart. She resisted the truth for a little while until all she could do from feeling helpless was to take action. To put herself aside and focus on them was easy and effortless. It was a natural choice to love them first. She could withstand the uncertainty as she learned to become the mother they needed. The disappointment and fear she experienced was in knowing that *she* couldn't give them everything. Feeling lost and overwhelmed with hopelessness and guilt—all mocking the person she used to be asking her, *'Did you really believe that life would be that easy?'*

Being their mother, made up just one part of her, yet it was woven in everything she did—everything that she was. Alba felt all of what they felt, from frustration to pure joy. The delight that came with being their mother filled her heart with countless heart-bursting moments. She welcomed those times when they drew her into their world, reaching her soul without a word. Constantly reminding her of what life was really about... L O V E! Their healing souls, arriving at just the right time. The love they gave changed her and taught her why she was meant for more. Life continued with new interruptions of struggle, which was when the fragility of life once again became her teacher. It opened her up to a new world that connects us all and grounded her as she became comfortable as a nurturer. It scared her as she was discovering who she was meant to be. Unprepared, she kept going, and throughout the adversities, she shoved down all the emotions that got in the way of putting them first.

It's been said that you choose how to react to adversities in life. It sounds logical, yet calm and reasonable choices occur in grounded moments. We are all doing our best to react to life appropriately, but what if life sucker punched you? Knocking you so off-center, it feels as though you're in a state of constant vertigo. Unable to catch your breath or stop the world from spinning. Forcing you to navigate through life in emotional chaos, refusing to accept the truth. Alba needed a reason why it felt as though few things in her life went as expected, and so she blamed herself. Could it be that her flaws, the parts of herself she turned her back on and hid from others were wrapped up in who she loved most? The idea that her sensitivity, that part of her that sometimes left her feeling misunderstood, was at the root of the chaos. This broke her heart. The intensity of emotion was inescapable, and she continued to resist, which brought more sadness. It was a devastating time, but even in the darkest times, she didn't give up because she was reminded that they *chose her*.

Like her mother, Alba abandoned herself and loved them more. Years passed with no time to pause until hope appeared. She learned to breathe again. The unfamiliar calm and slow pace uncovered more than what she was prepared for. The overflow of it all was too much. She kept it inside, unable to ask for help, as her heart was hurting. Dimming her light to cope with it all for far too long. On some of her best days, it took everything within her to get out of bed and get through the day. Moving through this time in her life was about pretending to be ok, sparing others of her suffering. Compromising her well-being and privately facing the dysfunctional person she had become. It was her resistance to trust that pulled her under, suffocating her as she grasped for breath—at times holding on while wanting to let go. Racing in slow motion, life became a haze of grey shadows of hope. Her thoughts would rush in and out like waves crashing, pulling her in and pushing her down. Feeling invisible, she was barely there, closed off from life, from love, from connections. Overcome with the reality of who she became as a result of how life had unfolded. Losing sight of how beautiful life really was, she became an observer of her own life, peering into a shattered window reaching for fragments of her dreams. Slipping into the sadness, the guilt, the disappointment, the doubt, comfortable with limits she chose based on fear. Alba questioned everything.

But what do you do when life is too much? When fear takes over, doubt creeps in and hopelessness settles into you like it was always meant to be there. How do you find the light to heal your broken heart to bring yourself back to who you are meant to be? She was losing herself and it scared her enough to let go of what wasn't meant for her, so she embraced her truth. She was freed from a dream that was no longer hers. Although she couldn't make sense of everything, she always knew she was blessed with love. The kind of love that fills and empties you; that builds you up and tears you down. The most important kind of love that steadies you. The love for her family and her children and learning to love herself was a part of her love story and who she was meant to be.

Alba was brave enough to choose herself—this is what saved her, and gave herself permission to heal. Without hesitation, she kept going and did not give up. Reflecting on the lessons she learned about the fragility of life her mother taught her, she realized it gave her what she needed. Alba knew that no one would get in the way of her loving the dark corners of her heart. With a thoughtful heart and a giving soul, she collected the broken pieces of herself; she stepped into the light with hope and courage. She shed the sadness, the pain, and the fear. She claimed her place and honoured theirs. She strived to give them *her* all. She looked inside and felt the joy that never died. She found her way, slowly, step by step with struggle and success, with resistance and love. Always with love, rooted in love, giving, and receiving with love. Her truth, her tragedy, her gratitude, her privilege, her hope she gave to them. With honesty and sincerity, with commitment and without expectations.

She whispers...
My darlings
My sweetnesses
My joys
My purpose

My life
My heart I give to you all I can, and seek to always find ways to give you more.
I see you
I know you
I honour you
I understand you
I respect you
I adore you
I love you
You I love, more than I love me, more than I love life. Together for always, together for-ever.

Determined and empowered by the heaviness of the past, she rose with grace. It gave her hope to take her life back and heal. She was open to the possibility that she would show others how to love themselves specifically with an awareness of their natural needs which makes them whole. This inspired her and strengthened her commitment to be better for her children and herself. She continued to grow and heal, which welcomed more into her life. When finally, there was an understanding she made with her heart that allowed her thoughts to arrive into a rhythm that served her best. It took time as all transformations do, but there was no rush, no competition, no finish line because she listened and trusted her inner knowing. Stepping into a new world with fresh eyes, she began to believe. Alba was open and eager to be alive again, appreciating the beauty and darkness of life. This was when her strength was tested yet again, but her little girl embodied the true meaning of resilience. She taught her how to face adversity with grace and discovered new levels of love. An unwavering love, the kind that can endure some of life's most frightening moments. A new perspective of the fragility of life gave her the courage to face each day with gratitude.

NORTH STAR

She realized that despite her fears—when traumatic memories appear unannounced and unwelcomed, her north star would calm her. Her north star was the harmony she felt from her family's love that she depended on in life when the world changed around her. Their love took her to many places and introduced her to the power she had within that would always carry her forward. The pain of their past would forever be overshadowed by those heart-bursting love moments that empowered her to feel with a depth that took over her heart. It's what gave her the courage to revisit the peaceful place in her heart where that little girl who took in the world with an intensity still lived. She discovered that it was about learning to listen to her heart, to be kinder to herself and to continue to self-nurture. She knew that her resilience was because of her sensitivity. That part of her, she believed was a weakness and sometimes left her feeling misunderstood, was, in fact, her greatest strength. It enabled her to become the mother her children needed, to appreciate the capabilities and the potential that lives within us, and to truly see how each of us takes in the world as a gift. This inspired her to show her children and those around her that they are so much more than they know. Experience taught her that life and all its beautiful imperfections maintain a balance that stirred her soul. The diversity of it all, the people, the places, the sights and sounds that breathe shades of colour into her life. This always brought her back to herself and who she was meant to be. To be their mother, to live a life filled with levels of love, and to light the path for others to know that their lives mattered.

Our children teach us how to love ourselves and one another. They are the love the world needs, and their shining light holds all of our potentials. Alba treasured their love and the life moments that shaped her. The memories, the lessons and losses, the heartaches and disappointments led to embracing her truth, and it saved her. She could see that, like her dreams, choosing to believe she mattered took time. She made a promise to herself that whenever she felt hopeless—she would never give up. She promised to love them and protect them, to give them the space to be exactly who they were meant to be. To show them that everything would be alright and that anything was possible. To tell them that she would always be there, always waiting to love them just the way they are. Her goal remained to remind them that they mattered and to tell them,

'Oh, my sweet one, you are love, and you are loved. May you receive the love you give in all the ways that matter. May your light always shine as bright as your true potential, and never forget that the things that matter to you will always matter. To be heard, to be respected, to be understood, to feel connected and to value your thoughts, ideas, and your voice. To love yourself is the greatest gift you give, most importantly to *your* children. To hold space for what matters to you. To be intentional with your attention is when your calm heart and open mind creates the purity of joy that survives and where growth lives.'

The Beauty From The Ashes

JESSICA RICHES
HAIKUS BY GRACE RICHES

The wound is the place where light enters you

rumi

It was 4 pm on Christmas Eve, and my family and I were on the first leg of a long-awaited extended family holiday. We were in London, England, exploring Christmas in Hyde Park, travelling on the tube, dining in pods by the Thames, marvelling at the magnificent holiday lights and enjoying high tea. I was in Harrods Department Store, described as a magical place, especially at Christmas. It was filled with glamourous people, luxury brands, smart doormen in green uniforms and spectacular decorations.

Yet I was on the phone with my husband, my then just twelve-year-old daughter a few feet away, unsure what to do as I was sobbing and dropping enough f-bombs to make Billy Connelly proud.

"Where are you? Are you near the flat? She has bled through her clothes again. I have no idea where we are or what to do!" My husband, well into the celebratory mood, had nothing to offer. He was a stranger in the same foreign land as me.

Since the beginning of our trip, my daughter had been experiencing a horrendous menstrual period that had her soaking through an overnight pad every hour. She was new to having a period and was still adjusting. She was uncomfortable, embarrassed and scared. All she wanted was to be at home with ready access to a bathroom with clean clothes, and I couldn't provide that for her. My baby needed me as she had never needed me before, and I was failing miserably.

So began what has become my daughter's journey with Immune Thrombocytopenic Purpura (ITP) and a revolutionizing of my relationship with her.

A life is to live
To choose, love, hurt, laugh, and live
The main point is, live

Grace is my second child and my only daughter, born 17 months after our firstborn son. I was thrilled to have a daughter. I am the eldest of three daughters and love nothing more than being with some of my favourite women, enjoying a long chat and yummy food. When the nurse confirmed I was expecting again, I felt overwhelmed. In one year, my husband and I had our first child, moved into our first home and purchased two businesses that we were running together. My husband worked long hours six days a week, and I was barely coping. *How on earth was I going to manage with a second baby?*

As I sat in the medical office with tears running down my face, I heard a distinct voice from God simply saying, "it's a girl." I was comforted immediately. A daughter? A girlfriend for life! I treasured those words and pondered them in my heart until many weeks later when the ultrasound technician confirmed at 37 weeks that I was, in fact, expecting a girl.

As a baby, Grace was of an easy disposition. She was content to watch her older brother move around; he would bring her toys and make her laugh. We were a threesome, having playdates with friends, visiting parks, the zoo and grandparents. Grace was the quieter one, content to hang back and observe.

And so went their childhood. Austin loved to learn but did not fit the mold of school. I was frequently in conversation with teachers and instructors because he wouldn't wait his turn, raise his hand, or would become quite upset when he had a conflict with a peer.

Meanwhile, Grace has always strived to be an exemplary student and a friend to all her classmates. She is helpful, cheerful, follows the rules and makes sure others do as well. Learning and performing the tasks required of her at school came quickly to her.

I had both kids enrolled in various activities—sports, playgroups, music classes. I felt it of vital importance that my children be well-rounded and accomplished. My husband was still working long hours to run our business, and I would be rushing to get a meal into us, then "hurry, hurry, hurrying," my kids into the car for the next activity. As I reflect back, Grace rarely thrived or shone in any of these environments.

She took courage from her big brother but never expressed enthusiasm, and as she got older, she began to push back.

Around eight years old, Grace was given the opportunity to attend horse riding camp, and she fell in love. She had found her passion. I engaged her with horseback riding as with everything else—commit, achieve, excel. Grace participated in a few shows, and I think I was as proud of the ribbons she won as she was! And yet, I began to become aware that perhaps my drive for my children to be accomplished was not as altruistic as I believed. Perhaps it was more about their accomplishments reflecting my success and abilities as a parent.

I was 37 years old and ten years into my journey of motherhood. I was wearying of my constant internal drive to be better and do better in my effort to create a life and future free of pain and heartache. I believed that if I worked hard enough and made wise decisions for myself and my family, we would somehow be spared any discomfort or challenges.

I spent time reflecting on this idea and came to see how much of my life had been driven by a need to appear "good," to meet all the expectations held by others of what a daughter, sister, wife, mother, and woman should be. I was striving for perfection in myself and that vision extended to my children. I was not allowing us to experience life fully, to try something new and quit if you hate it, or to belly laugh at a misstep instead of criticizing.

As I began this awareness journey, I watched my daughter grow from a child into a tween. I desired to reach out to her and share what I was learning about being a woman and embracing life fully. I realized that somewhere along the way, Grace had determined that she was better at dealing with her challenges on her own. She rarely shared her difficulties with her dad or me; we knew only because she would withdraw into herself and her room. She was like a turtle, retreating into her shell, with only the look of aching pain expressed on her face. While I would try to comfort her, there was little I could do because I couldn't reach her. I realized in my efforts to support and encourage my children, I had instead isolated my daughter's quiet yet proud spirit.

Sometimes life is hard
But you must push back harder
This is your purpose

On our return to Canada after our family holiday, I brought Grace to our family doctor, thinking only that her iron levels must be depleted after seven days of intense menstrual bleeding. The bloodwork showed low iron and ferritin but also showed dangerously low blood platelet counts. Grace was seen by a pediatrician at our local hospital the day after the bloodwork results. I tried to stay calm while my husband and I discussed how much to tell Grace. We talked extensively with the medical staff, discussing Grace's health history and symptoms. The pediatrician thought it was likely her platelets were low because of a virus but ordered follow-up bloodwork for two weeks later as a precaution.

The two weeks passed uneventfully. I was walking the dog in the forest when I saw an unfamiliar doctor's office calling. With my heart pounding, I answered my phone and was informed an appointment had been made for Grace with a pediatric hematologist four weeks from then. Shortly after, Grace called me from school complaining of a headache. She had participated in gym class, developed a headache, then fell asleep, head on her desk, for the following two periods. This pattern occurred a few more times before we connected that her low iron and platelets were the cause, and she was unable to take part in any activities that required physical exertion.

When the appointment with the pediatric hematologist finally arrived, we were packing for our annual March Break trip to Florida, while still wondering what was happening in Grace's body and what the next steps would be. My husband took the day off work, and we drove into the city.

We sat in the colourfully decorated pediatric office, with babies and young children surrounding us. With her half-shaved head, my almost teenage daughter sat sullenly with earbuds, listening to music. I paced. My husband compulsively tapped his toes.

Finally, Grace's name was called, and we approached the door of the doctor, knowing our lives were about to change but with little idea to what extent. The hematologist told us

Grace had ITP, Immune Thrombocytopenic Purpura. For an unknown reason, her immune system had begun to attack and destroy her platelets, resulting in low blood platelet counts. Platelets are required for blood to clot, and so low platelet levels cause the person to bruise easily, may cause excessive bleeding and make the person vulnerable to internal bleeding from minor bumps and bruises. There is no cure. The treatments have varying effects of success but are only temporary.

Grace had to cease all physical activity immediately; her platelets were so low that a simple bump to her head could cause spontaneous internal bleeding. We were told children 12 years and under see this condition resolve itself within a year, 90% of the time, but since Grace was already into puberty, she might not fit into this pattern. The doctor reviewed the possible treatments and advised regular monitoring of her bloodwork and symptoms. He gave us a list of all the activities she was unable to do when we arrived in Florida the following week.

Upon our return from Florida, due to the stay-at-home government orders, we could only have phone conversations with the hematologist. Grace's bloodwork done prior to our departure had shown much healthier platelet levels, so the doctor monitored her according to her symptoms. Grace's menstrual bleeding had continued to be at a normal level and coming roughly every four weeks. I was lulled into believing that this frightening time might be behind us.

The week leading into Easter, Grace said, "Mom, my period had been getting lighter but has gotten heavy again over the weekend." We called the hematologist. While on the phone with him, Grace mentioned that she was feeling winded walking up the stairs. He told us to head to SickKids Hospital in Toronto immediately. At this time, hospitals allowed only one parent to accompany children, so I needed to be calm and brave for my daughter without my husband's supportive presence. I said a prayer, called my husband to inform him of the developments, and we packed overnight bags just in case.

We made the drive to Toronto in record time. The highway and city were eerie in their emptiness. We were admitted to the ER, awaiting whatever would come next. We joked nervously, trying to keep each other's spirits up and avoid dwelling on the uncertainty of what was happening in Grace's body. Bloodwork was done, and we were informed that Grace's hemoglobin levels were very low, as well as still low platelet and iron levels. We saw several different specialists and were given two options—give Grace a steroid treatment and be released home or be admitted and give Grace an immune globin treatment. I had no idea what to do. There was no time to research our options to determine the best possible plan. My daughter was ill, and I needed to do what was best to get her well.

I asked the hematologist what he would do if she were his child. His response, "do both treatments." So that is what we did. Grace was given an IV treatment of a steroid with the hopes that it would suppress her immune system to slow the platelet loss. She was admitted to a room on the 8th floor with a couch for me to sleep on and our own bathroom. The medical team of five staff came in to introduce themselves and explain what would happen over the next number of hours. Grace was given a wide variety of snack options and happily chose chocolate milk and cereal. The immune globin treatment began via I.V. late in the evening, and I sat in wonder at my daughter, who seemed intent on enjoying the snacks, attention and full control of the TV remote.

I don't know how but I slept that night, rousing a few times to peek at Grace and ensure she was comfortable. We were woken the next morning by the staff doing their rounds. Grace had completed the immune globin treatment, and now she was to be monitored for side effects. We ordered breakfast from the hospital, Grace loving that she could order whatever and how much she wanted! I was able to leave the room to buy tea and some favourite snacks from Starbucks.

We spent the day together, the staff coming in and out to monitor her and ask questions. I took notes and kept family members updated while Grace was content to watch TV and order food when hungry. Grace was doing well, but the doctors were still concerned about her hemoglobin and platelet levels. There was much discussion about the possibility of a blood transfusion. We went to sleep Thursday evening, hopeful of being discharged the next day.

Friday, we woke eager to find out if and when we could go home. It was decided that she would require a blood transfusion before discharge. While waiting for the transfusion to begin, Grace noticed two pigeons asleep on a neighbouring windowsill. It was Good Friday; the streets of Toronto were empty. We wondered at the normalcy of birds sleeping unworried on an 8th floor windowsill while our world felt like it was turned upside-down.

Watching my daughter receive the blood transfusion was surreal. It felt both life-giving and life-taking. I was grateful to have the hospital's care and our provincial health plan, yet it seemed like a violation watching the blood of a stranger stream into my daughter's body. Grace was unflinchingly brave through all of this. She was courteous and patient, never complaining. In some ways, I felt like it was a do-over. My daughter needed me, and this time I was able to help her, to advocate for her on matters large and small, to share the simple joys of salt and vinegar chips with Starbucks green peach tea and "The Goldbergs."

Our journey with ITP didn't end when Grace was discharged from the hospital. Trips to SickKids are a part of our life, although thankfully, no more overnight visits have been necessary. Grace has become a pro at getting her blood taken, and she has her favourite lab to visit. The hardest part for Grace has been that she was unable to horseback ride until her platelets were at a healthy level set by the hematologist. The possibility of a fall off the horse was too risky. By August, the roller coaster ride of platelet levels and accompanying restrictions had worn her down. She was feeling hopeless and discouraged. I was gravely concerned about her mental health. I reached out to her hematologist to find out what options might exist for treatment. We were told of two possible medications. The first one was covered by our provincial health plan but would suppress her immune system and the second option was extraordinarily costly but explicitly made for ITP. I pursued approval of the use of this medication with our benefits company, as well as a grant administered through the hospital, and thankfully was able to have the costs covered. She began the medication, and today, Grace's platelets sit at a healthy level, and she has been back horseback riding for several months. We continue to pray that this condition will resolve, but in the meantime, Grace can live without restriction.

During this struggle, all that has mattered is Grace's physical and mental health. Although I wish with all my heart that Grace did not have this condition, I am eternally grateful that I have been given the opportunity to spend many hours with my daughter in challenging situations. This has provided the chance for me to lean in and pay attention to what is important to my daughter, to learn what she needs and values. I have had the opportunity to fight for my daughter instead of fighting her to be what I think she should be.

This journey has often felt like a fire raging through our family. Our long-awaited family holiday to England was fraught with concern and mishaps. My daughter's grade 7 year was marred by uncertainty and pain; her grade 8 year began with weekly appointments at the lab and warnings to her teachers about her physical limitations. Perhaps the most painful was watching my daughter shrink from a sassy tween full of life into a teen who was hurting and withdrawn from the world.

Yet, like flowers that bloom only after a wildfire, there is beauty that emerges from the ashes. The sorrow we have experienced makes my daughter's smile and laugh more beautiful, the ordinary moments in life with family are imbued with significance. I still catch myself almost daily trying to control the future, managing and manipulating our lives to avoid difficulties. Then I take a deep breath, and remind myself that all we have is the moment we are in; regardless of if it is filled with pain or joy, every moment adds to the beauty of our lives.

You May Bend But Never Break

NICOLE RECKER

"When are you going to have kids?"

I never thought one question that society deems normal would leave me with so many mixed emotions.

If only they knew what I had gone through. But they didn't, and it was just a question.

In reality, one in four people will have a loss in pregnancy.

I was very unlucky to be one of the four. Life had a greater plan for me.

UNKNOWN TERRITORY

In 2015, my boyfriend and I decided to try for a family.

In July 2016, I found out I was pregnant. *Holy crap, this is happening!*

I surprised my boyfriend with a photoshoot to get action shots of him on his dirt bike. The photographer asked that we stand back to back and write what we loved about each other most on a chalkboard. I can't remember what he wrote, but I had written, "you're going to be a dad."

We turned around, and his reaction was priceless. We were so excited, and our imaginations started going. Nine weeks in, I began to have cramps and thought I had a miscarriage. We went to the hospital; the Doctor did an ultrasound to listen to the heartbeat but said the baby was still small, so we may not hear it. She did a pelvic exam and said everything looked okay. Finally, she did some blood work to check my beta HCG levels and said, "if I call you, it will be very likely that you, unfortunately, had a loss.".

I came home and prayed. My sister and I were inside waiting while my brother-in-law and my boyfriend were outside.

My phone rang.

I immediately felt my heart hit the floor. My sister ran to call my boyfriend. I never saw someone run so fast. The doctor asked if I had someone beside me and if I was sitting down. I said yes. She then said, "I am so sorry to say, Nicole, your beta HCG levels have dropped greatly."

Doing everything I could to hold back my tears, I replied, "Okay, thank you for calling me back so quickly." I hung up the phone, ran to the bathroom, and hit the floor. I can still hear the cry that came out of me that day. I thought I was to blame; maybe I vacuumed the carpet the wrong way.

My boyfriend hugged me so hard. He whispered in my ear, "Nicole, it was nothing you did, take a big deep breath. I've got you." H*ow could life be so cruel?* I thought to myself.

I then began to think about everyone I had to call to share the heartbreaking news too, wondering how I was going to find the words.

I had many hard days ahead, but I put one foot in front of the other and continued on.

HOPEFUL

Six months later, we tried again. I found out I was pregnant. I felt many uneasy feelings. Do I get excited, do I not? This time I wasn't sure how to tell my boyfriend. I decided to buy a six-pack of donuts with a note inside that read, "you better eat up Daddy; Mommy can't be the only big one this summer!"

We told our parents and our siblings, but that was it. Everyone else could wait until I was 12 weeks or after our first OBGYN visit.

Everything was going well. We arrived at our first OBGYN appointment, and they couldn't find the heartbeat. " I should be able to hear a heartbeat," the tech said. She booked me for an urgent ultrasound. The radiologist came to the door, and without shutting the door, he said, "sorry, there's no heartbeat." Wait, what!? He just made it seem like I lost my keys. The tech didn't even show us the screen to understand. She just said, "okay, here is the way out. I'll give you a minute, have a great day."

I just looked at my Boyfriend, with so many questions.

The comments from professionals and people in general, were piercing to the skin. My Doctor said, "if you have another loss, we'll think about fertility issues then. Just keep trying. Maybe those weren't meant to be." "Are you sure you want to have kids? You'll lose so much sleep, and they cost a lot." I couldn't believe what I was hearing.

The lack of empathy some professionals had blew my mind. I have a history of working with doctors. I get it, we can't have every medical professional crying at the bedside, but it is essential to recognize that the person being told the news is a human being who is going through great loss and should be treated with a little compassion.

I experienced three weeks of uncertainty as my symptoms stopped with me, on some days, feeling completely normal. My mind and heart held on to hope while my body did too.

My body then decided to let go. April 18th, at around 11:00 pm, I woke up to intense pain. I felt like I was being paralyzed. I couldn't move. I told my boyfriend we needed to go to the emergency room. I told him it was happening again. He replied, "Nicole, we don't know what's happening. Let's just get to the hospital."

On the drive there, the sharp pain continued with every breath. The only relief was grabbing onto my thigh and my boyfriend's hand.

We reached the emergency, and the nurse called me into the triage area. I broke down and started to hyperventilate. "Ma'am, take a big deep breath. I need you to explain what is happening," she said. "I think I'm having another miscarriage," I replied. She had a nurse, an OBGYN, and a gynecologist greet me with a wheelchair. My boyfriend walked beside me, but they wouldn't let him in the room. I insisted that I couldn't go through this alone. They offered a nurse to hold my hand.

"Everything is just sitting here at the opening of the cervix. I am so sorry, but you're going to feel a slight tug, and I'm going to remove all of it," the doctor said.

I held onto that stranger's hands and cried.

"I'm going to tug, and you're going to want to jump as it's your body's natural response," the doctor continued, "please try to relax and stay laying down." He pulled, and I immediately jumped up, and I, unfortunately, saw everything on the table. I broke down and demanded for them to bring my boyfriend into the room.

A couple of hours later, we left with nothing.

FAITH

Throughout this journey, I've had difficult obstacles, lots of fear and uncertainty. But I've also learned so much.

It would have been easy to give up on my dream of having a family. I mean, come on, at one point, the entire world felt like it weighed me down. What I realized is that I had to trust in myself. I had to be my own voice in a quiet place. I believed something good had to come from all this heartache. So I let myself feel what I wanted to feel. Some days that looked like doing nothing but crying, going down to the river to throw rocks while screaming as loud as I could, crying, looking back in my rearview mirror and praying for a baby to look back at me.

Then my boyfriend and I found a new doctor. She heard our story and said, "that's all I need to hear. We'll start fertility testing." Instantly tears streamed down my face in relief. It was as if I had been drowning for so long, and someone finally threw me a life raft.

Never having gone through fertility testing, I wasn't aware of the emotional and mental rollercoaster this would bring. I was picked and poked, test after test. I felt like I was a science project. In the end, we were told, "you are both normal, no fertility problems." I thought I would feel relief hearing that, but after everything, I wanted an answer as to why I had my previous losses. But some things happen without reason.

I decided to feed my mind faith, truth and a whole lot of love. Your mind only knows what you feed it.

I focused on myself and healing after the hardship. I opened up by being vulnerable, choosing to do things I've never done. Allowing myself to just be. Feeling what I wanted to feel, without a time frame of when I should feel okay.

I felt counselling would be an appropriate thing to help me feel stronger mentally. I was my best friend and worst enemy in the same sentence some days. I learned by letting go of my own beliefs and being vulnerable, and sharing with others when it was a comfortable place for me that so many others had gone through very similar pregnancy and fertility situations. Slowly I learned loss and infertility weren't topics people often spoke about.

The hardest part was accepting that I had no control over my situation. It didn't matter how much I wanted it. I couldn't choose the outcome. No matter what, I had to let what was going to happen happen. Having a loss in pregnancy feels like you're watching someone break into your car right in front of you, and no matter what, you can't do a single thing. You just have to watch them take what's yours.

I believe my journey to becoming a mom made me a stronger being as a whole. I continued to remind myself that I owed it to myself to keep trying because the weight of regret was something I was never willing to live with. The pain of continuing to try for a family while dealing with the unknown was easier for me to face than thinking of giving up. I wouldn't be able to live with the what if's.

What if I tried longer?

What if I have no children and die alone?

I was not willing to roll over and give up! I deserved to give it my all and to continue going until I held a baby in my arms! My intuition kept telling me to keep going and not give up. I trusted it so deeply. Hope. Faith. Resilience. Persistence. Never give up. These are the words that got me through the next part of my life.

NEVER GIVE UP

I got engaged, married, and arrived back from my honeymoon when I realized I was about three weeks late. I couldn't bring myself to do a pregnancy test. I had so many emotions. Every part of me wanted to be pregnant, but I was also terrified. I built up the courage to do a test. I was pregnant. Immediately I didn't want to get excited, but something in me felt different.

I decided to surprise my husband. I told him that we were going to go down to the river and take a picture. I told him I would write "fall in love" on a chalkboard and take a picture.

There we were, at the river, the exact spot he had proposed. I set up the video camera and hit record. I walked back to him with the chalkboard hidden. I turned it around, and it read, "you're going to be a dad." He looked at me with tears in his eyes, his voice cracking and asked, "really?"

I booked our first appointment at the doctor's and cried when I heard her say, "Nicole, you're pregnant."

We arrived at our eight-week ultrasound, and I was a nervous wreck. The technician said, "you've got a healthy baby there. Everything looks great." I cried so hard in relief. We left feeling so grateful.

GRATITUDE

Be life a Buffalo.

In the wild, when a storm comes, all the other animals in the wild run away from the storm. By doing this, the storm chases them. Making them stay with the storm longer. While the Buffalo are the only animals that choose to run directly into the storm. Making the Buffalo pass through the storm faster.

Being like a buffalo, I realized to focus on things I can control rather than what I can't and sometimes running head-on into the most difficult times in life is what needs to be done.

These were the wise words that my Midwife shared as I came closer to the end of my Pregnancy.

This pregnancy was a complete fairy tale. I remember hearing our baby's heartbeat for the first time and crying tears of joy every time I had the opportunity to listen to it. I recorded every single one.

As my body grew, I looked at myself in the mirror differently. My heart was filled with gratitude for all the special moments I had gone through. The ones I was soaking up in the present and the future moments to come—even the ones where I wanted to puke at the smell of taco meat cooking.

I hugged my belly. I spoke and sang to my baby. I drank something sweet to feel my baby move around. I enjoyed the feeling of movement when my baby would stretch and kick me in the ribs. The best was when I was sleeping, and my husband would have his arm across my belly, and our baby would wake us both up with a kick that would move my husband's arm. I enjoyed feeling everything. So much so that I decided I wanted to have a natural delivery. I wanted to experience it all; after all, I never knew if I'd get this experience again.

Of course, fear and negative thoughts tried to sneak in during my delivery, but I knew they weren't serving me. I had doubts, and for split seconds, I wanted to give up during delivery but I reminded myself that I had gone through worse to receive less. This pain was a good thing, and I knew the best was yet to come. I used the power of meditation, motivational quotes, and breathing through all the hard stuff. I never lost sight of the goal.

I was finally going to have *my* family.

INNER STRENGTH

I learned that we have to surrender and stop fighting against the challenges and instead rise to them as they were made to make us better. You see, sometimes the biggest gift in this lifetime is on the other side of all of the heartbreak. All the uncertainty. All the unanswered questions. All the pain.

It was worth it for me, and I would do it all over again, knowing I would hold my little man at the end. I am forever grateful that I chose never to give up and continued to have hope because the best thing that ever happened to me, besides my husband, was having my son.

I got what I always wanted, *my* family. I successfully had my son naturally. The inner strength I never knew I had, was found. I did it. Wow, I beat it all. I choose never to give up, and this was my victory moment.

With this victory moment, I met someone I knew nothing about.

The new me I was becoming. I learned so much about myself in the three days after having him than I did in my entire life. People ask me what the biggest thing I learned when I became a Mom was.

Patience.

Patience to get things done in a different order than what I had in mind.

Patience with myself to heal when I was ready, not when I wanted to be ready.

Patience with this little human who had just been birthed to an entirely new world. He needed the most patience and love that I never knew existed. My inner guidance struck back with hope, hope and trust in me and the process.

The love between a Momma and Child is the most instant love I have ever felt. That exact moment he squirmed right up to me, and I looked right into his eyes, and he looked back at me. Immediately a love bigger than I ever knew possible. My entire world is complete with my Family.

Caring for my Son, seeing him smile for the very first time. Hearing all of his little sounds, learning all of his cues, all of his different cries. Learning through all of the new stages. Hearing him call Momma and Dada, having him run around with my Husband and hearing them laughing those incredible belly laughs together, hearing his voice, watching him make sense of this world we live in along with a million other things was truly so rewarding.

I find comfort knowing the babies from my previous pregnancies have been reborn with my Son.

Which to some may sound a little woo woo.

But, hear me out. Somethings you just can't explain.

My first loss was on August 20, 2016.

My second loss was on April 19, 2017.

Wyatt was born in the year 2019.

I choose to believe that the dates I lost those other babies, 20th and 19th, were no coincidence as Wyatt was born in 2019.

Despite feeling like I have the entire world with my family, being a Mom has its challenges. Mine tend to come with mental challenges where I fight two people in my head. The one part of my brain, the Mom, the me who gave it my all to hold it together and still feeling like I didn't do enough. While the other part of me reminds myself never to complain, as there was a time in my life where I would truly give anything to have what I have today.

This one afternoon, my heart overflowed so much that I cried in the car on our drive back from our adventure. Why?

Because I have a massive grateful heart for this little man.

We are a very loving family. We hug, say I love you and give kisses all the time. We express ourselves and have the longest conversations even though with my son, not all of the words are actual words. We tell him powerful messages, teach him positivity, self-worth, confidence, strong beliefs in himself and to love wholeheartedly.

On that drive home, I told him how I was so proud of him because he did such a good job on our adventure. He said please and thank you without being asked, he got in his seat without a meltdown, and he listened so well the entire time. As I'm looking back at him in my rearview mirror, I paused for a moment and said, "I love you so much, baby."

He looked back at me in the mirror and said, "I love you, Momma."

My heart exploded, and tears rolled down my cheeks. When I was pregnant, I would wonder how his voice would sound, and my goodness, I struck gold with him.

Having him taught me the unimaginable strength one can have. Which was a reminder in some situations that I can be in control.

So continue to have faith and remind yourself, "I can, I will, end of story!"

Trust in the Journey

SUSAN BAKER

What could have been a story of loss,
became a story of triumph.
What could have been one of despair,
is now one of hope.
What could have been a tale of giving up,
is now a story of pure potential.

Susan Baker

Becoming a mother, you learn it's all about love. Sometimes, you don't get to choose when you love, how hard you love, or how deep. And sometimes, the love you feel actually hurts. Sometimes, great love ends in great loss.

This is the story of each of those loves—of how I became a mother and of what shaped me into who I am today.

If ever I hesitate in my telling of this story, it's because of you, the reader, the receiver. Managing *your* response to this story used to be why I didn't share; I knew I could only handle my own.

But time is a gift, and it is because of this that I can share one of the most beautiful and raw parts of my life: my journey as a mother. It is in sharing that we realize that we are not alone, that our stories matter, and that they are, most definitely, what bring us together.

This is the human connection—*our* human connection—and our connection as mothers.

On some level, our stories nourish the soul in all of us.

LOVE WITHOUT CONDITION

I am the mother to three children. Two of them are with me in this life. One of them, I had to *give back.*

That was ten years ago.

Already a mother to Andrew, my first-born, I was excitedly pregnant with our second—our sweet baby James. My husband and I were happy and healthy. I had no worries—with my background in holistic nutrition and years of living a healthy lifestyle, why would I think otherwise?

But about halfway through my pregnancy, we learned that one of James' kidneys was small. Many ultrasounds later, the doctors determined that his kidney wasn't developing properly, resulting in very low amniotic fluid levels. My husband and I were given options; we chose to see where fate—or faith—would take us, even if it meant kidney transplants, infant dialysis, and a childhood full of visits with doctors.

I spent every other week being monitored in the High-Risk Pregnancy Unit at Mt. Sinai hospital in Toronto. James was a perfect size and shape, except for his kidney. I carried our baby a full 38 weeks, then was induced so that the specialists could see exactly what we were dealing with.

James' delivery was healthy, and he was beautiful, but his cry at birth wasn't normal. It wasn't what we expected to hear; it was stifled, and he was struggling. Within seconds of his entry into the world, he was whisked away to the neonatal emergency room. I held him only for a moment. He was unable to breathe his own breath; the x-rays showed that not only had his kidney not developed properly, but his lung capacity hadn't either. His lungs were a healthy size, but their surface area for breathing was under-developed—a potential complication of low amniotic fluid levels very early on in pregnancy and something you can't see in utero.

We waited hours for an update.

Finally, after countless tests, it was determined that our precious baby boy had two major organ systems in failure.

James lived in the NICU, and for seven days, so did we. He was born at Mt. Sinai, but when his case required the best in the field, we were transferred to Toronto's Sick Kids hospital. It was traumatic, surreal, and was the longest week of our lives.

I remember feeling like time stood still within those blank hospital walls—like the rest of the world carried on while we spent long hours waiting, praying, and wondering.

In the end, it became apparent that there was nothing we could do. We couldn't 'fix' our baby—not even with all the medical experts and treatments in the world. We were faced with the reality that, for James to truly experience 'living', we had to set him free. We had to remove the ties that were keeping him bound to his physical body—his physical life—so that his soul could truly live. It was one of the most excruciating decisions we would ever have to make as parents.

On that seventh day, we set him free.

We left with an empty car seat.

It was all very surreal. And very, very sad.

We were in shock and disbelief.

It's hard to make sense of these things. I stopped trying. And I know it's the same for people who have endured miscarriages, still-births, or the loss of a child who could never be conceived. Things don't go the way they're 'supposed' to, but I'm learning that this is sometimes how things go in life.

That one week taught me my strength—as a person and as a mother. I didn't know it then, but I see it now. It taught me a strength I didn't know I had, a strength I would need—one that would serve me in the years to come.

I am a stronger mother for both of my children because of having had James—my beautiful, sweet baby James.

LIFE AFTER DARK

Six months later, Abby was conceived.

I cried with relief the day she was placed in my arms, breathing.

She was and still is the light that shone through the darkness. She reminds us to have fun, to play, to laugh, and that there is always joy available, even after pain.

Abby was named after a complete stranger—a curly-haired redhead who bounced into my husband's life one day on the subway home from work. "Hi! My name's Abby!" She introduced herself and proceeded to tell him all about her life, as her mother smiled on.

She lit up my husband's day. She brought tears to his eyes. He later retold the story and said, "If we are fortunate enough to have another child one day, we will name her Abby, and she will be pure joy."

We had just lost our sweet baby, James. Our Abby was merely a flicker of hope in our hearts.

Ten years later, she still is that bright, shining light. Pure joy. It seems inherent—like she was born that way. There's no expectation—she just is! Our light after dark; a light that I hope never dims.

Abby is a beautiful child, inside and out. She loves life and takes it for what it is. She embraces it with a genuine desire to give love and be loved in return.

She is happy, compassionate, strong, funny, thoughtful, and has a spirit all her own! It is like watching a beautiful flower blossom under all conditions. She is so deserving of all of the joy that she puts out into the world.

Abby adores her family—her mom and dad, grandparents, cousins, but maybe most of all, most especially, her brother, Andrew.

She has a loyalty to her brother that never wavers. She enjoys him, defends him, and admires him. And he loves her in return. Her care and respect for him is a gift.

None of us knew that their relationship would mean so much, in so many ways—then, now and in the years to come.

But life is full of things you can never predict.

THE ROAD LESS TRAVELLED

I didn't know autism before I knew Andrew.

Andrew was my first.

With the beautiful, naive outlook of a first-time expectant mother, I embraced the pregnancy—all the feelings, the whole experience. My energy was great, I gained a healthy amount of weight, and I glowed!

A textbook pregnancy, labour and delivery, Andrew arrived naturally at 41 weeks, 9.5 pounds. He was a gorgeous baby boy. He was breastfed till 18 months, fed homemade baby food, unvaccinated, and on 'all the right' supplements. I was a purist, an idealist. He had tons of time outside, in nature, and had minimal TV.

Andrew was perfect and wondrous, and I didn't know any different.

By age two, he was showing signs of atypical development. He wasn't speaking. "He'll be a late talker," people would say. He studied everything. "He'll be a scientist," they would say. He had a serious, 'etheric' nature. "You were just like that!" they said.

What others saw as atypical, I saw as unique. I embraced my child's individuality; I didn't need to label it. But by two and a half, we were in the pediatrician's office.

I had just lost James. I remember saying to the doctor, "Please tell me that I'm just a grieving mother who is overly vigilant, and that I should go home and have a glass of wine." But he didn't say that. Instead, he got his checklist out and red-flagged us for autism.

I never suspected, nor expected, autism. I just didn't.

By the time Andrew was three, we were in early intervention services, and by four, with a new baby (Abby) in my arms, we were given a diagnosis of severe nonverbal autism.

It was given like a life-sentence.

We felt distraught, overwhelmed and alone.

What they *didn't* give us with the diagnosis was perspective or any kind of hope for the future—something like:

- *Always presume competence. There is more to your child than meets the eye.*
- *Be open to all of life's possibilities for your child. Trust your gut.*

- *Most importantly, but hardest of all: Never give up on your child. Not ever.*

We would end up finding these truths on our own.

One day, in the thick of our autism diagnosis and the emotional ride that goes with that, it all just hit me. I stood in front of the tree planted in James' name, watching Andrew laugh at the wind, and I sobbed. I cried for the loss of a child and the loss of a childhood. But in that next moment, when I looked again and saw Andrew joyfully experiencing life, and I thought of James' one week, something profound occurred to me:

Maybe people don't need to be fixed to truly experience living.

And so began the journey of learning to support our child, not 'fix' him; support him so that he could thrive being who he is—who he is meant to be. What a beautiful and challenging journey that would end up being.

TRUST IN THE JOURNEY

Autism parenting is not easy, and there is no road map. I have yelled, sobbed, cursed, and felt overwhelmed beyond function. Autism is not a "one size fits all"—no child is—and so it is a constant recalibration of where you think you're going, based on where you are now.

But some of the greatest challenges were my own. Getting over what my child *should* look like—what he *should* be doing or how he *should* behave. My own desire for perfection and control, over time, was eroded by my deeper desire to love my child unconditionally.

Certainly, there are significant and very real challenges. Still, the greatest growth was my own. Learning to let go: letting go of expectations of how I thought things should go. Being open to seeing things differently. When I opened my eyes, lived in my heart, and made decisions from my gut, incredible things happened. Moving away from living in fear, worry, and lack, to living in trust, belief and love. This is where the possibilities exist. This is where the solutions show up, and the extraordinary happens.

From this open place, one of our greatest discoveries was made: a communication method that would change everything for our family and our child, finally giving Andrew a voice. A story all its own, it became possible for us to finally get to know our child. We have had the chance to learn Andrew's thoughts, feelings and opinions, and does he ever have brilliant things to say!

In one of the most beautiful, full-circle moments of my life as a mother, I sat with my child and watched him spell out, letter-by-letter, these words:

Mom
Feeling overcome with a beautiful feeling
of love and gratitude for you
and all you have done for me
all these years
I am forever grateful.
How you had the patience and perseverance
is a gift I will keep close in my heart always
Here's to so much ahead for us.

He left me speechless, moved to tears.

A beautiful gift; the gift that is Andrew.

—

The opportunities for growth in this life are infinite.

If I tried to recount what I have learned, it would be pages. But if I look back, even before my life with children, these are the lessons that showed up for me, over and over again:

Accept. Accept that life will look different than you expect. Accept that there will be pain, sadness, challenge, and tons and tons of joy if you choose to see it.

Be open. Be open to a life that takes you in a direction you can't predict or that you didn't know existed. One you certainly can't control.

Trust. Trust in the process of life. In the journey of living. And live it. That's all you need to do.

—

We all have a story. If you had told me that this would be ours, I'm not sure that I would have taken it on! But life is like that; you never know what lies ahead.

Our story is still unfolding, carrying with it many gifts along the way. In many ways, ours is a story of perseverance, resilience, and certainly one of trust. It has brought my husband and I closer together, when it could have torn us apart. I have learned my strength, but I have also learned that it is okay to feel weak. I see my courage, but I also see the bravery in accepting help from others. I have embraced vulnerability like a friend because I have felt the joy that it brings being real and authentic. And I continue to practice being in the present moment because that is the only place where life truly happens.

Part of me feels anxious in the unknown, in what lies ahead. A bigger part of me, though, trusts in the journey. My spiritual beliefs about life allow me to receive this life, and my story, with a knowing that it is all as it's meant to be — that my life is absolutely meant *for me*.

I don't know what happens next or how this story ends. What I do know for sure is that this is *our* story: real, beautiful, and lived. It has brought us to exactly where we are supposed to be—and it always will. Exactly where we are today.

about the authors

JANICE LAI YEE NG

Janice is a dedicated mother to two boys. She loves all things creative and adventurous. You can count on her whether it's baking, sewing, or skydiving. Most of all, she loves creating deep connections with people; to inspire and be inspired.

Dedicated to all the strong women in my life who, through their actions and words, supported me and built my confidence to be a whole person. Last but not least, to my husband who saw me through the changes of motherhood and to my kids who pushed me to believe in myself again.

IG: @joyfulhearts.co | joyfulheartsco.com

MARNIE SIGMAR

Marnie is a work in progress! After completing her Master's at Queen's University, Marnie found her love of non-profit work at Inspiration Café in Chicago. Her work is focused on people experiencing homelessness, domestic violence and people living with AIDS. She loves to travel and, on one adventure, fell in love with the children at a small orphanage near Mombasa and founded an organization to support it. Marnie loves her family fiercely. She loves being a mom, partner, daughter, auntie, sister and friend. To say she is grateful for them is an understatement. Though Joe is nineteen now, in her heart he will always be her boy and she will always be his mama.

To my family—Your love means everything to me. To Joe—I love you more than you can imagine. The gift of you in my life is what I treasure most. There are no words for how grateful I am for you. You are pure sunshine. To Alex—I can't keep track of all the ways my life is amazing because of you. I am still crazy in love with you and am deeply grateful for how much you love Joe and I. You are the best papa.

IG: @dragon.fly.clay

LESLEY ANN FARIA ADAMO

Mother, wife, teacher, artist, design-enthusiast, and creative soul at heart. Lesley spends her days inspiring the young minds of her students. She has been a dedicated teacher for the last fourteen years; and finds much joy in the creativity that she is able to inspire everyday. She is a dedicated mother and wife, and loves spending her time exploring, playing and travelling with her family and friends; soaking in all of their time together and making memories.

"I am Found" is dedicated to my girl. My why; my Ava. Thank you for making me a mama. Thank you for bringing me back home to myself and showing me a love I never knew possible. Mama loves you more than you will ever know.

Special acknowledgement goes to my first loves and nurturers; my amazing parents, Manny and Marie. Thank you for showing me the way and for being an example of what it means to love unconditionally and stand by those you love with the most unwavering commitment and strength. You've set the highest bar.

Lesley.Faria@gmail.com | IG: @lesleyfadamo

RUTH SCHALKHAUSER TOWER

Ruth believes in a world of infinite possibility, abundance, and love. Through heartbreak, she learned to follow her heart and chose love post-divorce when she got married at a drive-thru chapel in Las Vegas. She is a yoga and meditation teacher, as well as a spiritual life and business coach, guiding spiritually-minded women to embody their life's purpose and leave a legacy.

Dedicated to my mom and grandmothers, who showed me true strength and love in motherhood, and my dad who set the example for heart-led leadership. To my husband, Ken, whose unwavering love and belief in me calls me higher. And to my incredible children, Beka and Connor, whose love and affection constantly inspire me to live as my truest self.

IG: @innerskyliving @soullegacyalchemy
FB: @ruthschalkhausertower | soullegacyalchemy.com

EDEN PEREIRA

Eden's passion is capturing memories through photographs. In 2019, she was blessed with having her first child. A gift that she had prayed for, for years. Though her pregnancy journey was one she longed for it was an experience that taught her what strength truly meant. She hopes that her story inspires other mothers and mothers-to-be the perspective that every woman goes through their own unique journey in becoming a Mom and to allow the experience of every moment.

To Santiago; thank you for choosing me to be your Mother. I am forever grateful that you have taught me what it means to be strong. To Felipe; my soul mate, you push me every day to be the best version of myself, thank you. Mom; thank you—you are my Superwoman. You have taught me what a perfect Mother should be. All the hard work and love you have given me has set me up to be the best Mom for Santiago. There are not enough words to express the gratitude I have for your strength and courage. Simply, thank you Mom! My family and friends; thank you for all your support and love throughout my journey to becoming a Mother.

IG: @edenpereira @edenpereiraphotography
edenpereira.com

STEFANIA TERSIGNI

Mother, wife, teacher, yogi, life coach, traveller, foodie and lover of life. Rewind eighteen years ago, Stefania married her highschool sweetheart at the age of twenty-three after graduating from teacher's college. Three years later her son was born and two years after her daughter came into the world. Life was wonderful and moving at lightning speed. Nearing her forties, she decided it was time to finally listen to the calling in her heart. Yoga, meditation and intentional living play a vital role in bringing alignment to her life. Stefania strives to live each day in loving awareness, grateful for the abundance of life's gifts and helping others to see the potential they hold within.

More than a Mother is dedicated to the loves of my life, my children Antonio and Gioia. Thank you for inspiring me to be the best version of myself. I love you more. To my husband Tony, for always supporting and motivating me. I count my blessings everyday for the life we have created together. Looking forward to the adventures ahead!

intentionsandpositivevibes@gmail.com
IG: @intentionsandpositivevibes

NICKI DI GRAVINA

Nicki Di Gravina is a loving wife and mother, as well as a Holistic Nutritionist. As an advocate for holistic wellness she has developed her businesses, fundraising initiatives and projects to reflect her commitment to helping others create a better quality of life. Her creative and curious nature led her to explore writing as a new form of imaginative expression.

Dedicated to my children Sofia and John, and to my husband Mike for being my north star. I'm thankful for my children's wise souls and all they've taught me. I'm especially thankful for my husband who has never wavered through it all, and continues to appreciate this beautiful life that we've created.

info@feedforlove.com | IG: @feedforlove
feedforlove.com

JESSICA RICHES

Jessica is a Jesus-follower, wife, mom, daughter, sister and friend, and she takes great joy and honour in each role. She seeks to live life fully, learn from her experiences, and share kindness with all whom she encounters. Jessica runs a business with her husband, and dreams of the day she opens her own coaching practice.

My deepest gratitude to my family for their ongoing love, grace and support. Special thanks to my sister Luisa for her excellent editing skills and many conversations acting as a sounding board. To my daughter Grace—thank you for allowing me to share our story, and forgiving me my many missteps.

IG: @jessicaanneriches

NICOLE RECKER

Nicole Recker is forever grateful for the opportunity and blessing to be a wife and momma. This role has led her to dig deep into personal growth and become the best version of herself. It has fueled her to encourage, empower, coach, lift and support other women. Nicole has this fire and determination to share her story so that she can spread hope and the importance of never giving up.

I would like to acknowledge my husband Andrew. I am forever grateful that our paths crossed because you're the best dad and husband. To my Son, Wyatt, I am forever grateful that you chose us to be your parents as you're a light in this world and you've completed our world. To my family and everyone else who has been on this journey, thank you for your unconditional love and support.

IG: @nicolereckersjourney | FB: @nicolecrecker
nicoledavis2.arbonne.com

SUSAN BAKER

Susan Baker is a mom, daughter, partner and friend. Susan is the author of Life, Love & Autism, an online blog that chronicles her family's journey of growth and challenge, including love, loss and an autism diagnosis. Susan is a holistic nutritionist and has been in the natural health industry since 2001. She inspires health in others through her online programs and social media presence. She loves good food, margaritas, and the colour purple. Susan lives in Toronto with her husband and children.

To Stuart, for your support, love, and all the laughs! So grateful for our partnership. To my three children, for making me who I am.

And to all the women in my life—every single one—for lifting me up along the way; thank you for being my community.

IG: @lifewithsusan | FB: Life, Love & Autism

susan@behealthyforlife.ca